Grandma Debbie

The Cradle of Life

by

Debra Cannamore Lee

Grateful,
Debra Cannamore Lee

Library of Congress Control Number: 2017911962

ISBN 978-0-692-95832-2 (Hardcover)

ISBN 978-1-980-69898-2 (Softcover)

ISBN 978-0-692-91443-4 (Ebook)

Cover design by Jamie Wyatt. Butterfly illustration created by Freepik.

Edited by Karen L. Tucker

Published in the United States

First Edition

Visit www.grandmadebbie.com

Dedicated to Mutt's Babies and My Three Gs

This book was written in
remembrance of my son Fatman.

Contents

Introduction

There is a time and a place for everything and everybody. Some things happen by chance, some happen because they are meant to be. It's amazing how even we can make some things happen. Destiny is full of timetables; it holds life and death within its hand. These are our stepping stones in life, moments in time that we can never replace.

Note: Some names have been changed to protect the individuals' privacy.

Just a Young Girl

I am sitting in my family room looking out my window at the tree tops as they have grown through the ages. This reflection of life takes me back more than four decades that have come and gone as so many of my loved ones have as they traveled through my life. They have left behind the precious memories of when we were all here together as a family.

At the splendid age of nine, I was just a young girl with a full future ahead of me and not a care in the world. Our lives were filled with and surrounded by the melodies of joy and pain that could be heard and felt amid the musical artists of Motown—singers and musical artists like Diana Ross and the Supremes, The Temptations, Smokey Robinson, James Brown, and Aretha Franklin. Songs like "Bring the Boys Home" spoke to our wishes for the soldiers who were fighting in the Vietnam War. Some of the songs, like the ballads of Marvin Gaye, even spoke to the era of our lives and an unknown future; the lyrics and beat of the songs were so strong, even I could identify with the love and heartache. This music sparked a passion in me for dancing. My favorite was R&B and good gospel singing.

We had a medium-sized family; our parents, Oscar and Laura Mae (Mutt), led a family of four boys and two girls. Nicknames were fashionable during the fifties and sixties. The oldest was Clemmie, who was called either Sunny or Sun June; followed by Rommie, who was known as Snookie Boy; and Oscar Jr., who was called both Pookie Boy and Tobey. Seven years later, I was born. It seemed as if they didn't try as hard with the nicknames of their last three children. They called me Debbie, and I was marked from birth as the strange one. Three years later, my youngest brother Kenneth (Ken) was born, and not even a year later—eleven months and twenty days, to be exact—my only sister Denise, called Necie, was born. My parents must have stayed in the groove of the love songs of the sixties to have gotten my little brother and sister that close together. We had a strong family resemblance as sisters and brothers, but we definitely had different personalities. All of us had our mother's mouth; our lips didn't close, making our mouths look like that of a cooing newborn baby. This was the first telltale sign we were Mutt's babies.

Our parents owned a lounge called Oscar's Tavern in the heart of downtown St. Louis on Biddle Street. For the sixties, it was a big deal that my father, a man of color, had a liquor license and served both black and white folks. Biddle Street was an interesting place to live; most of the businesses were black owned and operated. These were the original street vendors. The block had an ice man, a coal man, a hot tamale man, and of course, there was the tax man, Mr. Meeks. This was a life full of ups and downs. My father later changed the name of his business from Oscar's Tavern to Laura's Lounge to keep up with the changing times and to expand their clientele. Later on, my dad opened a restaurant next door to their lounge for my mother and renamed the business Laura's Lounge and Restaurant.

Three to four people worked in the lounge. Ms. Thurlee was the main barmaid. Our families were so close; we considered ourselves to be related and addressed one another as cousins. My mother always opened the lounge on Saturday mornings so that my dad could sleep in. My brothers, my sister, and I would help with the household chores and tend to his needs. We cleaned the house, washed the car and the dog as well as made our father's breakfast. Everything had to be done before he left to go to work at two o'clock to relieve my mother at the tavern.

Other employees worked in the restaurant to help them out. My older brother and I both had to clean up the tavern on Sunday. As the middle child, I had the easiest job: washing the glasses. Every glass had to be washed by hand using the swish brush. I turned each glass back and forth until it was clean and then rinsed it. Excited to be helping, I thought I was a really big girl and doing something huge.

Biddle Street was a strip of businesses and homes, mainly two- and four-family flats. People lived above the businesses, a common custom in downtown St. Louis. We lived right across the street from both of our parents' businesses in a two-family flat. There was a trucking company next to the tavern and a red church across the street. The pool hall was a few feet from the church.

My paternal grandfather, Reverend Melvin Lee Cannamore, was a minister and pastored Stranger's Home Missionary Baptist Church with his wife Sister Janie Zone Cannamore, the first lady of the church, which was the next block over from the tavern. This made us a well-balanced family between the church and the tavern. My grandfather passed away in 1963. His son, Reverend Herman Cannamore, was then ordained as the pastor of the church. The new church was built directly across the street from the original church to accommodate its growing membership. Those were the good old days when people could worship and afterward get a good home-cooked meal without leaving the church. The new church had a kitchen and sold food on the weekends. They also made good, old-fashioned ice cream. I would watch in a daze how the old church women would take an ice pick that was sharper and harder than any blade or knife to break those humongous blocks of ice used to churn the ice cream. They would give you a good stick with that ice pick, too, if you got in their way. My parents worked in the tavern and restaurant Monday through Saturday, and we were in church every Sunday.

I didn't mind going to church because my uncle was the pastor. He allowed me to go freely in and out of his study. I didn't have to pay for any of my meals. Sunday was our family day: we worshiped together, we had dinner as a family, and we had fun as a family. I sang in the choir and was a junior usher; all the kids had to participate in some capacity within the church service. You didn't have a voice or a choice. We did what we were told to do. We usually could get away with stuff everywhere else, but not in church. My favorite part of service was attending Sunday school. My big brother Pookie Boy and my cousin Wilbert were Sunday school teachers. I was in awe of my brother's knowledge and speaking skills. He had the ability to captivate an audience with his charm and charisma. It was one of his God-given talents. On the other side of the fence, Wilbert had to practice all the time, having us over to his house to "play church" when it was his turn to teach that week.

Stranger's Home Missionary Baptist Church had a magnificent and enchanting choir. I felt like everyone in my family could sing but me. My cousin Eula Perl would sing with an angelic expression on her face. Her voice was so beautiful that it touched the spirits of the children, causing them to shout when she sang. My cousin Herman Jr. could sing and play the drums and piano. When Eula and Herman Jr. got together, you would think you were at a live gospel concert. We were a wild and joyous, spirit-filled family. Some days, the young adult choir members would pretend to be shouting and dancing, making fun of the women in the church. The ladies would shout so hard when my uncle preached that their wigs would start sliding off, especially when the Word got inside of them. Those Christian women did not play; you would look up, and all of a sudden, one of them would make a mad dash toward wherever my uncle had mounted himself to preach. They would throw handkerchiefs at him and attempt to run up to the pulpit. The ushers had their hands full, but they had a no-nonsense attitude. I think they had eyes in the front, back, and side of their heads. If an usher caught you chewing gum, she would come marching down the aisle and grab you by the hand. If you were lucky, she would bring you to the back of the church and give you a good pinch. But if you got that mean, hard-looking usher, she would take you outside and give you a good spanking, and no one would say a doggone thing. Grandma was on the Mother's Board, watching everything. Between her and my momma, we would get it again once we got home. Embarrassment was a sure way to discipline us and maintain control. Under no circumstances did we want our friends to see us get our butts tore up.

In 1968, my parents were ready to move on to their next undertaking, so they started looking for a new home and ways to expand their business. They looked at a lot of homes. My favorite was the house with the sun porch on Adelaide Street. I was disappointed when they did not purchase that house. They decided to buy a duplex on Penrose in North St. Louis. They took no input from me. When the time came to move, I did not want to leave 1424 Biddle Street. I had a horrible feeling that something was going to happen to us. I never told anyone about this feeling, and in my childlike despair, I kissed the walls, furniture, and everything we were leaving behind goodbye.

Once the move finally happened, the next phase for my siblings and I would be to attend our new school and begin making new friends. My parents, meanwhile, made a lot of updates to the house. My father had the basement refinished into a lower-level living quarters; a brick patio in the backyard and awnings on the windows added to the exterior of the house. It really was a beautiful place to live. However, only a short time later, my dad purchased another building to relocate his business and family. The building had living quarters above it, so once both the business and family moved into it, Penrose would be made into a rental property.

There was something about relocating to North St. Louis that was unsettling to my spirit. I did not like the new school nor was I fond of the people. North St. Louis was being integrated at the time with blacks, but the whites started moving out. Realtors were steering black families into the North City neighborhoods as they moved white families out to the suburbs. However, there were both blacks and whites in the same neighborhood until the early seventies. The North Side was a beautiful place to live—clean, with lots of flowers and trees. Businesses lined both sides of West Florissant Avenue all the way into the heart of downtown St. Louis.

My mother had her household well organized. She made breakfast each morning and got us off to school. Once we were gone, she would leave and go help my father run the business. Miss Emma, the housekeeper and babysitter, had moved right along with us. She spent many nights with us until it felt as if she lived with us. She made our lunches and dinners as well as cleaned the house. Miss Emma took the summers off because we were shipped to Earle, Arkansas, to stay with Aunt Effie D, our great-aunt.

Aunt Effie D was our grandmother's younger sister. There is a caveat to this story. My grandmother did not raise my mother. The story went something like this: My mother had a real bad case of thrush when she was six months old. Aunt Effie D took my mother from her sister, who was my mother's biological mother, because she was too young and did not know how to take care of her. So Aunt Effie and her husband, Uncle Wick, raised my mother as their own child. Then my grandmother had a sister who passed away during childbirth, and she raised those kids with their father. This was one hell of a story. Since those kids, my mother's cousins, called our grandmother Aunt Leo, we called her that too, even though she was our grandmother. What a way for a grandmother to confuse her grandchildren, but things like that often took place back then without any explanations given. My grandfather on my mother's side lived right there in Earle too. We never got to meet him before he passed away. (My father's parents lived in St. Louis and had died in the early sixties. My grandfather had a heart attack while shaking the hands of the choir members as they entered one by one into the choir stand. He was dead before he made it to the hospital. Grandma died a few years later.) As soon as the summer was over, we were shipped back to St. Louis in time to go back to school. That year, I was anxious about going back to the new neighborhood because of the change and the anticipation of the unknown.

It felt awkward having to change schools. All the kids wanted to test the new girl. Bryan Hill Elementary School was a mixed school then. However, the majority of the students were white. I really didn't know if there was a difference at first—at least, not beyond skin color. On Biddle Street, there had been no white children. Some of the business owners were white, but we only saw their children when they worked in the stores. I never felt any prejudice there because my father and family were so well respected within our community.

Living on the North Side gave me my first real life lesson in prejudices based on the distinctions in skin color and texture of hair. My family members were of various complexions and had different textures of hair, and I loved them all. My mother was light skinned and my father was dark skinned, so our family was a beautiful rainbow.

My brother Pookie Boy had a lot of problems when we moved to Penrose. He was a novelty to his new neighborhood, and his peers wanted to try him. Either you fit the bill or paid the bill. Pookie Boy wasn't accepted from the beginning because he had transferred from Vashon High School to Beaumont High School, which were rival schools. Our parents dressed us nicely, and we always had lunch money. Subsequently, jealousy and envy were ready to have their way with us. He had to fight on the way to school, through high school, and on the way home from school. I could not understand the fighting and how mean the other kids were toward us and any other new students. Shoot, we all lived in the same neighborhood. However, there was a point in time when blacks hadn't been allowed on the North Side and couldn't even enter Fairgrounds Park. So we didn't fit in, and as children, we didn't get why not, although I didn't really try to. Fortunately, my younger sister and brother were too little to have any problems. Eventually, we all found our place: good, bad, or otherwise.

There was a happy medium that allowed us to accept the North Side as our new home. It wasn't long before I was transferred to Harrison School due to the rezoning of our school district.

*****

A few years later, Pookie Boy enlisted in the Air Force. We were so proud of him when he graduated from basic training. He stood tall, black, and handsome in that Air Force uniform. Not long after Pookie Boy's graduation from basic training, my cousin Eula Pearl was sent to collect me and my younger siblings from school. I was only twelve, but I knew something was wrong. My teacher spoke briefly with Eula Pearl and directed me to come with her and my cousin. I kept asking Eula Pearl what was wrong, but she would not tell me. When we got in the car with her, she told us Mutt was waiting for us at the hospital. When we arrived at the hospital, I noticed that my mother was crying and a nervous wreck. She hugged us especially hard as she told us that our father was in the operating room. She had made him go to the doctor because he was coughing up blood. During the examination, the doctors determined he had lung cancer and he required emergency surgery. I had an inkling that cancer was a bad thing by the way people looked when they spoke about it. What I did not know was how cancer destroyed lives.

My mother brought her husband home where we would care for him. One of my father's favorite sports was hunting rabbit, squirrels, and quail with his brothers and friends. So when he got home, he immediately went straight for his awesome gun collection, which he began cleaning. It worried my mother because she was afraid that he would hurt himself, but he was in control. Everything became so blurred, like we were living in a dream. It was really hard for my mother trying to keep the business going, running back and forth to the hospital, and keeping tabs on all of us at the same time. My adolescent life was rapidly coming to an end because I had to share in the household responsibilities.

Although he had been weak when he came home, as time went on, it seemed as if my father started to gain his strength back and was recuperating quite well. After a lot of therapy, he could walk with a cane. He was alert. But the cancer was attacking his body with a vengeance. As the disease progressed, a hospital bed was brought in and a nurse came several times a week to check his vital signs and to administer his medication. The doctors advised my mother that my father should be placed in a nursing home, but that is not what black people did. These were the times when we took care of our loved ones at home. That is exactly what my mother did. He stayed at home with his wife and children. I had heard the saying, "once a man and twice a child." This is so true; I saw my father's transformation back to a child right in our own home. Even though this was his physical condition, he wasn't giving in without a fight. The cancer was aggressive and debilitating. The doctors had given him six months to live. Six months ... they had to be wrong. I thought to myself, "How could a doctor tell you how long you had to live?" He was talking about my daddy; he had to be crazy or something.

Then his health took a particularly bad turn. His body started to break down day by day. He lost movement in his right hand, and not long after that, his right leg began to go numb. He eventually had to stop driving, and within weeks, he went from using a cane to being dependent on a wheelchair. Our world was spinning too damn fast, and it felt like nothing could stop it. Where was God, where did he go? We needed him, we needed him! I don't know how he did it, but my father remained strong in spirit and in mind.

During this time, we still lived on Penrose Street just one house away from the intersection of College Avenue. I used to sneak up the street because I wanted to have fun like the other kids. But boy, oh boy, when I would return home, my father would have fallen, need to be changed, or be hungry. I would feel so bad and realized that I was in this for the long haul. My mother and I made pallets on the floor by his bed so that we could be right there when he needed us. My mother would give him injections of morphine for the pain. It was hard for her as she prayed for God to heal her husband while she watched him fade away.

We watched our father, my mother's husband, become totally dependent on us to care for his every need. When the cancer started eating at his brain, he was no longer able to tell us what he wanted. For some strange reason, as the end was approaching, I was the only one who could understand my daddy. I had to summon a whole new level of love and strength as his health declined. I was forced to do things that a child should not have to do for their parent, but this was my father, and I had to help my mother care for him. In my mind, I entered another world when I had to bathe and clean my own father, like he had done for me when I was an infant. I was just twelve years old; I still wanted to go outside and play with the other kids.

*****

My childhood gradually became a distant memory. Along with helping my mother with the household chores, I tended to the needs of my younger brother and sister. During this time, people actually dealt face to face with each other, with businesses staffed to assist their customers. I would go downtown to Pulaski Bank to pay the house note and to each utility company to pay the gas, light, and telephone bills. This was real life. It was good for me to learn this, but not fair, by any means.

When big changes are about to happen in our life, God prepares us. Sometimes I would go and visit other churches with my friends and their parents. One Sunday I visited Olivette Missionary Baptist Church with my friend Kayla. Her family lived in the red house on the corner of Warne and Penrose. On this day, her grandmother had questioned me about my grandparents, so I told her my father's parents were dead. She told me never to say "dead"; instead, say "expired." Then on September 26, 1969, the phone rang at night. At this point, my father had been back in the hospital for about two weeks. It was one of my uncles asking to speak with my mother. When I asked how daddy was doing, he said he was just fine. I gave my mother the phone. I must have drifted back off to sleep. The phone rang again and woke me up. When I answered, it was a lady from the hospital. She asked to speak with an adult in the house, but when I looked for my mother, she was not at home. She asked my age, and I told her that I was twelve. The nurse went on to tell me that Mr. Cannamore had just expired. I smiled for a moment as it came to my mind what Kayla's grandmother had said at church. But then I just started screaming and crying, and who knows what happened to the phone. Later that night, my mother and other family members came to the house. That is when I found out that my mother, God bless her, had already left for the hospital before the nurse had called the house.

I went downstairs to my room, wanting to die right then. I loved my father so much. I was a daddy's girl who he had spoiled rotten. I would get ten to fifteen dresses for school, go to the beauty salon, and always get my way with him. I could not imagine having a life without him. All kinds of thoughts were going through this young girl's head. Something started to take over me, like hurt and fury filling my heart. It didn't take long for me to recall my uncle telling me that my father was doing fine. I resented him for lying to me. My daddy wasn't alright, he was dying. I remember blaming God for taking my daddy away from us, and then I started running away from life. I began to run from myself and from those who loved me and toward the unknown.

I don't know which is the most overwhelming—having to say hello or having to say goodbye. One hello can open up a new life; it can turn our lives upside down or right side up. Saying goodbye could be for a short duration or it could be final; it, too, can impact our lives to the point of no return or give us freedom to embrace life again. My father passed away on a Friday in September 1969. As a young girl, I coexisted in a space of time between here and there, yesterday and today, afraid of tomorrow, full of joy yet coated with sadness. I was faced with the loss of my protector and provider, the man who had held my life in his hand. My father had a smile that would light up the world and the strength to tear it down, coupled with the love to give it peace. Yes, my father was my hero, and one of life's hard realities had pierced a hole straight through my heart.

I had been as close to my father as any daughter could be. I did not love him more than my mother, but it seemed that way. At the same time, my mother had focused more on my brothers and my baby sister. She always told me that I had ways like my father, and I must have had his mouth, too, because she could not stop me from talking. It truly got on her nerves. I had always had an outgoing personality, but with the additional responsibility, I started to blossom quickly. Bear in mind, we were raised around older people, who often referred to me as a "wise child" or one who had been here before. In laymen terms, I was ahead of my time!

As the summer came to an end, so did our days that had been full of happiness. Our family had experienced our first life-cycle explosion. Then one of my brothers got into some serious trouble, which caused my mother even more pain; the worry was written all over her face. My mother was a gorgeous woman. Her beauty was not just physical, but it radiated from within, through her smile and her touch. Once my mother, who had a heart of gold, touched someone, he or she was never the same. An amazing and talented woman, she loved life and lived life fully. She loved her family with everything she had. There was always a strength about her that commanded respect. My mother was such a stunning lady whose illuminating smile would dazzle you with an element of surprise. While she endured a lot of hurt and pain in her lifetime, she managed to overcome and live through it. Women of that day went through a lot; however, they kept quiet about everything no matter what their struggles. There is an old saying, "if walls could talk." Women's secrets remained locked up in their minds and hearts along with the past pain, hurt, betrayal, and all the love they had received and given. Prayer and faith were all they had to hold onto. There were no self-help books to guide them; all they had was God and his word, the Holy Bible, to show them the way.

It had to have been just as hard for my mother to lose a husband as it was for us to lose our father. My mother had always loved to drink beer for enjoyment during her free time after work or on the weekends. Now, she would use the time to cry about not having her husband with her. She would cry where only her God and her family could see the tears and prayed a fervent prayer every night. My mother would kneel at her bedside and say the "Our Father" prayer out loud in faith and hope that everything was going to be alright. Her devotion fueled my continued belief that two hearts truly joined in love can never be separated.

As the decade of the seventies rolled in, I began to evolve with the music and live the lyrics in my mind and heart: "Run Away Child," "Sitting on the Dock of the Bay," and "Color Him Father" were some of the songs that told my story. When I lost my father, I felt my options were taken away, and numerous fears found a place to rest deep within my soul.

Derby

Almost three years had come and gone since the death of my father. Derby had been my daddy's personal nickname for me. I took his death really hard and became an angry teenager. I blamed everyone for his death. I didn't know the road I would travel would rearrange our lives. This is where the prayers of my mother, great-aunt, and grandmother would play a big part in my life. I had always heard words like grace and mercy, but they would also talk about having guardian angels over them. I had no idea what those words meant at that time. But later, if I found myself in unfamiliar territory with no exit signs, the lightbulb would come on as I remembered those words. Then I would repeat every word that I had ever heard prayed.

My run had begun. I was running nowhere in particular. People ran behind me, on the side of me; there were people in front of me who I had not met. Some stayed longer than others on this never-ending ride. I knew I would end up somewhere sooner or later.

In the summer of 1972, I had begun to date an older guy. I was trying to be grown-up before my time, which cost me dearly in the long run. I did not tell him the truth about my age; I was fifteen but told him I was seventeen. I pulled it off because I had the body of an older girl, but I didn't have the mind of one. I wore my hair cut short on the back and sides, a sassy look that gave me the edge I needed to pass off as a mature-looking girl. When I met him, I was wearing hip-hugger pants and a popcorn blouse. The young girls and older women wore hot pants, sizzler dresses, hip-huggers, wet look leather, and sandals that laced up to the knee. The wrong dress would get you attention you didn't need and take you to a place you didn't want to be; I was dressed to go and no one could tell me to change. I spent the night with a friend, and we went over to her cousin's house. My mother had given me permission to spend the night with my friend; however, she was unaware that we were going out. At the time, it seemed like a harmless thing to do, but I knew it was wrong and went anyway. Her cousin was having a party, and we only had to pay fifty cents to get in. People were sitting on the couch, holding up the walls, or dancing. It wasn't long before a dark-skinned, nicely dressed guy came over to talk to me. We had what I thought was a good conversation. Well, I thought it was, but I really didn't know the difference; it sounded good to me. He said he worked for the government in downtown St. Louis at the Mark Building. I thought I had hit the jackpot: a nice-looking, sharply dressed, dark-skinned man with a good job. So we exchanged home telephone numbers. We talked on the phone every chance we got. I would go over to my friend's house to see him and invited him over when my mother was not at home—a huge mistake. Sometimes you make decisions that will cause you to take the long, long way around with a twenty percent chance of making it through.

*****

Well, we called ourselves "dating," and then the unthinkable happened. He persuaded me to have sex with him. I don't know if I did it to make him happy or because I longed to have a man in my life again. The loss of my father had caused fear and loneliness within me. Somehow, I thought that if I gave him what he wanted, then he would love and protect me from the world. A sweet and innocent virgin I was no more to be. After a few ooooohs and aaaahs, some pain, some noise, it was over in about five minutes. This act with no climax, a point of no return, and no emotional ties moved me from a being a fifteen-year-old girl to a fifteen-year-old woman. That was August 13, 1972, and there was no sweet hangover. Six weeks or so later, I was sick, throwing up. In that moment, I realized the error of my ways. We talked on the telephone one night, and I mustered up enough guts to tell him I had not been feeling well and had been vomiting. He said to me, "You know you pregnant." I was in shock and crying; the emotional roller coaster ride had begun. How would I tell my mother? What was I going to do? Where would I go? Most of all, how in the hell did he know? Well, somehow, he knew what he had done. When I missed my cycle, I lost it. In the seventies, a pregnant teenager was an outcast. It was an offense that carried more time and weight than murder or drug charges. At least, that is how it felt once my parents' friends, my friends' parents, my relatives, the church, the school, and the kids in the neighborhood all got done with me.

Six months later into my pregnancy, my mother found out; she was so hurt. I couldn't help thinking about how society dictated that girls could not do what the fellows did. When you put your all into one guy, all the upsets and odd things that happen make you vacillate from happy to unhappy, to a lake full of tears. In pleasing a man and giving your physical self, your self-respect is lost forever to a no-win situation. You lose yourself, you lose the trust that everyone had in you, and you miss out on your teenage years and young adult life. You lose the boy, your friends, and the favor of your family.

My mother found out from my big brother Pookie Boy that I was pregnant. I had told his friend and his friend told him. I thank God for my brother; nothing in the world could separate the love and the bond we had for each other. He was always there for his little sister. He had a good talk with me to let me know he would be there for me; I was bringing a life into the world. He also kept my mother, great-aunt, and grandmother from killing me, although they still didn't make it easy for me. They made my life hell, and I cried the entire nine months. I just wanted to go somewhere and never return. I had all kinds of thoughts about having this baby and running away. But the bottom line was that I didn't have anywhere to go and I was too afraid to run away. My mother wanted me to see what disobedience breeds and to understand the long-term effects it would have on my life. She was being tough on me out of love, but I thought she straight up disliked me for being pregnant.

My status in life went from ten to zero. Everywhere I went, people would stare and say things like, "She is too young to be pregnant," or "Look at that baby having a baby. Oh, she is going to end up being a little whore." You name it, I heard it. No one would let their girls play with me anymore. My play days were long gone; only teenage girls that were not pregnant could play and have fun at fifteen. I was about to enter full physical and social womanhood. All the ugly words and false predictions only made me stronger. I was determined with a vengeance to love, be loved, take care of my child, and make it. We would have the good life like all the other girls, and I would make everyone eat and swallow every word about the prophesied life they had formed for me. I found a fighting spirit inside me that I had never tapped into before. I was the daughter of Oscar and Laura, and that was enough for me. I also knew a little bit about God and his love for me, which I held onto during the trying times.

I had seen other girls my age and a little bit older who did not have babies go through hell. They lived in the streets and had to do things for boys to stay at their houses—guys who were much older than them. Some of them were in abusive relationships. This was not something that was prevalent in the seventies, but the few girls you heard about or saw made you know that you did not want that life. All I had done was let someone talk me into giving away my virginity. I was not about to leave home and let someone take my life away from me too. This was my rationale: I had made a mistake and would rather let my mother drive me up the wall and follow her rules than end up on the streets. All I wanted was the best for my child. It was evident I would take this parenting ride alone. I did not want the father of my child after I got pregnant. He felt that if he could not have me the way he wanted, he would not do anything for me. That was fine with me. After making the decision to join the Marine Corps, he left in December 1972. I remember listening to Aretha Franklin's song "Call Me When You Get There." Who was I fooling? The truth of the matter was I didn't know where he was going to start his tour of duty and I knew he wouldn't be calling me anytime soon. He had made his decision to move on without me, and even though it hurt me deeply, I had to move on with my life.

Then the day arrived. I was lying in my bed as big as a balloon when I started having cramps. The pain was unbelievable; labor pains were kicking my butt. I knew I had to make it upstairs to the kitchen to get the phone (cordless phones were uncommon in the seventies). When I made it upstairs, I called my mother at her job to come home. She hurried home, called a cab, and off we went to DePaul Hospital on North Kingshighway. This is when she taught me a real lesson, letting me know I would be on my own. After she registered me at the front desk, she waited until they prepped me and got me into the labor and delivery room. Then I looked up and my mother was gone … vanished. She left me there all by myself to deal with the labor and delivery of my child. I went through those horrible labor pains alone. Mothers in the seventies were something else; they showed real tough love. They would make you stand on your own. I had made my bed hard, and she made sure I was going to lie in it.

After being in labor from two in the afternoon until after midnight, my little bundle of joy took his first breath of life. When the doctor told me, "You have a boy," and the nurse brought him to me, I had no idea what to say or do. I had brought a life into the world—my son. I experienced a lot of emotions for a sixteen-year-old girl, but there was one clear feeling and that was that I loved my baby. I didn't know what the hell I was going to do next, but I knew I had to love and nurture him. I can recall the first time my son cried; when the doctor made him cry, it was a strange and beautiful sound. It was surreal to me. We had a five-day stay in the hospital. My son spent four of those days in my room. This was what my life was going to be like. I was his mother. It was me and my baby, and at that point, nothing else mattered. I was going to do everything in my power, regardless of my age, to make a wholesome life for my family. My son would never have to want for anything or anybody. Motherhood stepped right in and took its place—yes, motherhood and a mother's love at the ripe age of sixteen.

When it was time to go home, my mother had a friend of hers pick us up. While my mother had been there daily to see her grandson, she still hadn't had much to say to me. Without a doubt, though, she was going to make sure I didn't miss a beat in taking care of her grandchild. It was a long ride home. My little sister and brother were so happy with the arrival of their new nephew. My little brother was going to have a real human toy to wrestle with and play ball with, and my little sister was going to have a live doll to feed, change, and, most of all, to love … what she had always done best.

After I came home from the hospital, I learned that a friend of mine who was my age died after having a C-section, but the baby had lived. I realized then how blessed I was. Although young and fragile, I was beginning my journey as a mother. I recalled an old church song whose lyrics spoke about the worst that could happen to a mother was getting a call that your child was in trouble. We lose our children to the system, the streets, and to death. The death of a child is the worst of all because it is final. All hope of them coming home, turning around, or being delivered is over. I could only think about my friend's baby growing up without her mother. It did not occur to me that her mother had lost her daughter. I only had the understanding of a sixteen-year-old girl, and the only thing I knew for sure was that as a mother, I had a son to bring up. The love and kindness had begun to flow back into my life. I learned a little more about

God, Jesus, and what prayers could do for me. The fight deeply embedded within me was previously untapped faith. That faith was only the size of a mustard seed, but I held on to it tightly.

I loved my baby more than anything in this entire world, and now I had someone who loved me unconditionally. It seemed like my mother loved her grandson more than her own kids. The birth of my son filled the voids in both of our lives. He gave my mother life after the loss of her husband, our father, and the loss of her son to the system.

My mother was overjoyed by her new grandson, although she thought he was too little because he weighed only six pounds, fourteen ounces and was sixteen inches long. While she allowed us to live in her home, she told me I had to work and go to school, and she would help me out with him. One thing was for sure—the way I had been left alone in the labor room, dealing with those horrible labor pains, I was not going to have any more sex or children. My mother and her best friend, Willie Mae, along with her three daughters gave me a beautiful baby shower. My son had everything … and I mean everything: clothes, bottle sterilizers, pacifiers, sleepers, towels, diapers, a walker, a high chair, and oh my God, yes, cases of formula! When my baby turned six weeks old, my mother bought me a 1973 Mustang—a dream car. She did not want us walking or trying to catch a bus.

I am so thankful to God I had a mother with values who realized her daughter had only made a mistake and it was her duty to ensure that I was a responsible parent and a good mother. In her wisdom, she realized I was only a young teenager who still needed love and guidance to raise my child with those same beliefs and values. However, she did not make it easy for me at all. She accomplished this by using the hard love method. Hard love lets you fall down and stay there until you get yourself up. This is when you come to the realization that you are not in charge. Remember the biblical story about Peter when he attempted to walk on the water? When the storm came and fear fell upon him, he called for Jesus to save him. See, my mother already knew who Jesus was and who she was. I was learning who he was as well as who I was. Pookie Boy would tell me that everything under the sun is the same, just a different time and location.

Having my son was very different from babysitting when I could feed, hold, and change the baby's diaper then go home. My son was there all the time. He would wake up crying in the middle of the night more than once. I had to change his diaper, feed him, talk to him, play with him, and then maybe I could go back to sleep. I had all the help I wanted in the daytime. My mother, sister, and brother would be glad to help, but when nighttime came, it was mama's (my) turn.

My son charmed the whole family. When he was four months old, my mother took him outside to get some fresh air. She was feeding him his bottle on the back patio when my cousin Joe stopped by to say hello. He looked at my baby, grabbed his little hand, and said, "Hey there, Fatman." My mother liked the nickname Fatman for her grandson because he was such a cute, fat baby. From that day forward, everyone, including me, started calling him Fatman.

I was so glad when it was time to go back to school. My mother didn't allow me much freedom; she made sure I knew I had responsibilities and wouldn't allow me to slack. As time progressed, I got a job because there was no way I was going to receive assistance from anyone. I attempted to finish high school, but as graduation approached, I was short on credits, having only earned a few credits while attending maternity school, and would not be walking with the class of 1975. I was reclassified and, along with the other students who were short of credits, had to wait until the next school year to graduate.

My schoolmate Linda, who lived around the corner on Lee Avenue, was also a teenage mother. There were other teenage mothers who had finished school on time, so they thought they were better than us. One school day, Linda and I had a deep conversation in the halls of Beaumont High School with tears bubbling up in our eyes. While we watched the other students walking around with pride, heads up high and chests stuck out, making plans for graduation, I looked at Linda and told her I couldn't do another year of high school. Even though I chose to drop out of high school and get a job, it was obvious to me an education was extremely important—always was and always will be. My plan was to get my general equivalency diploma (GED) and go to a trade school.

This was when I first decided that I was going to go to college and be somebody. I had been in school long enough to know how to think, make a decision, and set a goal. What I didn't know was how long, how hard, how lonely, and how painful the journey would be. Fortunate to have the support of my family, I wasn't going to leave home anytime soon.

In and Out

During the summer months before I had gotten pregnant, I had worked part-time at Neighborhood Youth Corps on 6600 Delmar and at the corporate office. I guess you could say I graduated because my next job was at Church's Chicken. The other students who had graduated had government jobs or worked at the gas company, the electric company, or, of course, the telephone company. I couldn't work those types of jobs because I didn't have a high school diploma. I worked hard at Church's Chicken, cutting up 200 chickens at a time in the freezer. Cold and afraid I was going to cut off my fingers, I didn't have a clue the long-term effects this would have on my health. I cut up the chicken, battered it, and tossed it into the hot grease to cook. Then I sold the chicken. That place was always busy. The crowds on Friday and Saturday night would drive me up the wall and back down again. People would come from nearby lounges and taverns and would be loud, demanding, and cursing you out. I remember when they sold six jalapeno peppers for a dollar. One of the customers had the nerve to ask me to rub the last pepper across my breast. Boy was I upset and hot. I couldn't curse him out because I needed my job. So I stuck it out.

The daytime rush hours were ok. We always had to keep enough hot chicken ready because folks came in hungry and could get upset at the flick of a switch. They needed to get their food and hurry back to work. I worked long hours, and closing was just as crazy: cleaning counters and the grills, counting inventory, restocking, and hosing down floors. It was an amazing thing to work eighty hours of hard labor just to bring home a $100 paycheck after the invisible, no-relation-to-me Uncle Sam got his share. I would be tired, wet, and smell like fried chicken. Then morning would come and it would be back to the grind again. My mother would keep my son while I worked and wash and iron my uniforms to help me out. I would work ten to twelve hours several days in a row, and since my mother knew I would not eat the chicken, bless her heart, she would send my little brother and sister in a taxi to bring me dinner during my long shifts. My mother and family were so good to me. One morning I was scheduled for an early shift. When I arrived, I noticed a person in a Church's Chicken uniform exiting the glass-enclosed lobby. We spoke then I proceeded to go through the door. To my surprise, the manager was on the phone calling the police as he had just been robbed by that man who had on the damn uniform and had just walked out the door. God became even clearer and real to me as I realized he had protected me again.

Something inside me knew it was time for a change. The world was waiting for me, so I resolved to get a trade of some sort in the least amount of time possible. I saw a lot of ladies my age get jobs in nursing home facilities as nurse's aides and further their education. They would work their way up to become licensed nurse practitioners and registered nurses. It would have made my mother's dream come true if I went to nursing school and became a nurse. My mother, more so than anyone, knew I had the heart and compassion to help people. I went through a training program to be a certified nurse's aide (CNA), another step up. Once I completed the training, I immediately started work at a nursing home in south St. Louis. I worked the second shift from two in the afternoon until half past ten at night. Another uniformed job, but I earned a few more pennies and was making progress. The key to all of this madness was having a job with a paycheck. Although too young to be working this hard, full time, as a nurse's aide, I was determined to not be on welfare. I wasn't a dumb girl; I only needed to finish my senior year of high school. I could learn and do anything, and I caught on fast. As a more visual person, once I saw how something was done or processed, I immediately locked it in. It was like dancing to me. When a new dance came out, I would get to the dance floor as fast as I could. Once I saw someone do the moves a couple of times, I had it down pat.

It benefited me that I spoke well and carried myself in a mature manner. Although I didn't like this job, I kept it because the bills needed to be paid. My mother didn't charge me rent or make me buy groceries, but I paid for day care, my car note, and clothes. I also liked to buy my mother beautiful things. I would always save my money. My mother taught us to make sure we had "mad money" stashed somewhere and to never give away our last dollar. I would buy my mother furniture, jewelry, and clothes, and I made sure my little brother and sister didn't want for anything. Money would always come to me; God had his way of plain old blessing me. My mother never complained about how many hours I worked. As long as I was taking care of my son and making some sort of progress, she continued to help me. But the fact remained that I was low on the totem pole at work, and it seemed as if a shift change was not in my immediate future. Usually my baby was fast asleep by the time I got off work. The only quality time I had to spend with him was during the early hours of the day. The time was precious for both of us. I would make him breakfast and get him ready, putting him on the bus for day care each morning except on my days off, which fell on doggone Tuesdays and Wednesdays. I was blessed to send him to Happy Tot Day Care Center, a great child care facility. My end goal was for my son to be proud of me.

I totally refused to let being a teenage, single mother catch me and tear me down. No way, not Mutt and Oscar's daughter. I continued to work at the nursing facility. It wasn't long before someone else bought the company and made changes. This was an opportunity for me to make another career move. This job didn't allow me to be at home with my child or go to trade school. I had to explore other options, so the job and career search was on.

I landed my next job by demonstrating skills I didn't know I had. Although it wouldn't turn into a career, it was a new job. A friend of mine, Tonya, worked at Spokane's Potato and Onion Factory. Referrals were always the best way to get a job. This company, housed in a warehouse off Broadway, packaged and shipped potatoes and onions to food markets and grocery stores locally. Who would have thought a job like this existed? The workers had to hang bags onto a speeding carousal, where the potatoes and onions dropped off the carousal into five-, ten-, and twenty-pound bags. It seemed like the carousal turned at fifty miles an hour.

Tonya had only been employed there a few weeks when she informed me the company was hiring. Quite a few people showed up for the interview. This was not a typical interview where you sat down with a person and had a conversation. Ditch that idea. They had us line up around this carousel, grab some five-pound bags, and start hanging them. The carousel was spinning like nobody's business; bags, potatoes, and onions seemed to be flying everywhere. It felt like none of the bags locked onto the carousal, so the potatoes fell all over the floor. This was a mad way of testing to see who was best fit for the job. The supervisors called us over one at a time to let us know if we had the job. Not only did I get the job, I must have knocked it out of the park because when I got there the next day, I found out they had let Tonya go the day before. They had fired my friend and kept me. When I called her after my shift to find out what happen, she said, "They told me I was too slow." She never blamed me for losing her job. She simply moved on to the next job, and we remained friends.

I worked my tail off hanging those bags for eight hours a day. I would be so tired from standing on the hard concrete floor; you'd still be hot as hell even with the loud fans blowing at you. I got so tired of standing, I made myself a stool with a barrel turned upside down and cardboard on top for a cushion. The stool was so hard, it gave me hemorrhoids. I couldn't win. But, again, you do what you have to do! This was the price you paid when you take the long way around, when your head is so hard that you don't or can't listen to others, and you think you can do things your way. The upside of this job was my hours were 6:00 A.M. to 2:30 P.M. Monday through Friday, so I could be home with my son in the evenings and weekends.

I knew I had to learn a trade of some sort, so I applied to the St. Louis Business Institute in downtown St. Louis as it was listed as a reputable school. I had made up my mind to become a keypunch operator. An in-demand field at the time, I could make decent money at it. It wasn't long before I interviewed with the school, and a few weeks later I got the call. Lord, I had been accepted. I was so happy and ready for the challenge. But along with this great opportunity, the school required a high school diploma before they would award a certification. Life is so unfair. As soon as you think you can move forward, an obstacle stands in your way. Time was not on my side, so my best option was to take the GED test. Even though I had made it to the twelfth grade, I took some GED classes to be on the safe side. Once I finished the classes, I had to wait for my testing date. God knows how to keep you humbled. My family prayed a lot while we waited. We prayed for me to pass the test, get certified, and find a good job. I had heard it was a hard test to pass, and if you took it and failed, you had to wait another six months to take it again. I was going to work my butt off to make this happen. When test day came, I was afraid of all the unknowns. The instructors told you when to start and when to stop. Every section of the test was timed. I am so glad I had taken the classes. As they say, "preparation meets opportunity." When the test was over, most of us thought we had probably failed. So I kept working and going to class at the St. Louis Business Institute.

Challenging as it was, I continued to work the day shift at Spokane so I could attend trade school in the evenings. My mother, sister, and brother were in my corner, and there was nothing they wouldn't do for me and my son. Fatman was their heart. He was the gift of joy from God after the death of my father. My son had all the love and nourishment any child could ever want from my family. Three weeks before graduating from my class, I was sweating bullets waiting for the GED test results. I needed my GED before I could get my certification. I did well in my class, testing in the top five. Certification required a minimum of 10,000 key strokes per hour; I was kicking butt, clocking 14,000 key strokes per hour with no errors. I got off work one Friday and went home because I only had class Monday through Thursday. When my mother told me I had received some mail, my heart started racing and my adrenaline rose. It had arrived—my yes or my no. I took a deep breath and started praying. Lord knows I needed to pass that test. I ripped open the envelope and confirmed that not only did I pass the test, but I aced it. My diploma would arrive in a few weeks. I could do nothing but thank God. I started to run through the house screaming, "I passed the test, I passed the test." I was jumping for joy and had everyone in the house jumping right with me and thanking God. God is so good, and he is always on time. I was the happiest person in the world. There was more work to do, but the window of opportunity had opened, and an overflow of blessings had poured through. *"So I will restore to you the years that the swarming locust has eaten, the crawling locust, the consuming locust, and the chewing locust, my great army which I sent among you" (Joel 2:25 NKJV).*

By the end of 1977, I had gotten a job at Electronic Data Systems (EDS) as a keypunch operator working the second shift. I worked there for about 4 months before I received a job offer from Washington University. It was more money with daytime hours. A nice place to work, I found the people to be friendly and the work easy. The only downside was the once-a-month pay cycle, which caused a long wait between paychecks. The more I had begun to make, the more I spent.

After about six months at Washington University, I got another call for a position at Sigma Chemical Company. The jobs were so plentiful in the seventies and eighties, and the pay was awesome. Sigma offered me more money and great benefits. Although it was working from 2:30 to 11 P.M., it was an offer I couldn't refuse. I had hit the jackpot. I would be doing billing and invoicing. I worked the second shift for around two years. I was learning the business and moving right along. They wanted to put a new shift in place and asked me if I would like to work from noon to 8:30 P.M. Man, talk about happy! This was a sweet deal, and I took it. Sigma was growing and had begun to leverage their business with technology. I assisted with the design format of moving from the keypunch cards to data entry. Then Sigma hired this white guy from Milwaukee named Lou Michaels. As director over computer operations, he took the computer side of the business to another level. A few years after he had come to Sigma, Lou landed a position as assistant vice president of computer operations at Roosevelt Federal Savings and Loan, located downtown on Olive. When he left Sigma, he offered three of the top-performing employees better job positions if we would come and work with him. He offered me a position as a computer operator. My coworker Bob, who I called Blondie because he had red hair and a blonde beard, was a computer operator who would be promoted to a computer programmer. And he offered our coworker Thomas an opportunity as program manager. I took the position without knowing the company had plans to move to Chesterfield, Missouri. I had just made my 90 days at Roosevelt when they made the announcement. We worked twelve-hour days, six days a week. Man, I was clocking some dollars then.

*****

Knowing the importance of education, I was going to make sure my child received a good education. It was always in my mind and heart to go back later and earn a college degree. My mother, still acting as my guiding light, was influential in the decisions I made concerning her grandson.

She was adamant that he should attend a private school and insisted that I would pay for it. She set my priorities. I lived in her house, so I still had to abide by her rules as well as take care of my personal responsibilities. This made me think about how far my son and I had come. I began to reflect about our life together from the moment of conception. It doesn't matter what happens to you during your life, from good times through bad, you will always go back to memories of your child's firsts. That first cry, the first smile, the first coo. The firsts will always bring joy into your heart and put a smile on your face that no one can ever take away from you. I cherish the first scoot, the first crawl, and the first time he stood up by himself. I can visualize my son taking his first step and then trying to take another with me holding his hand. That's what mothers and fathers do: we hold their hands, take care of them, teach them, and protect them with everything we have. We watch and mold them through day care, preschool, and school; we are their best cheerleaders in everything they do or say. I can remember when I first realized that my baby could read. You know how children always want your undivided attention when you are talking on the telephone with someone else? Well, one day, I was sitting at the kitchen table talking on the telephone when he came over to me carrying his little book. He jumped up onto my lap. He was used to us reading together and me reading nighttime stories to him. So I read a line or two, and all of a sudden, he said one of the words. He was able to sound out some of the words; my baby was reading. I was so thrilled with amazement, I hung up the phone and hugged him so tight and told him how much I loved him and how proud I was of him. My son had his mom, his very own advocate, who would be his champion for life! Then we read some more stories together, such a precious and sweet time we shared.

Before I knew it, his preschool days were coming to a close. We celebrated his fifth birthday; he was growing into such a big boy. He started kindergarten at St. Paul Lutheran School. There had been only a couple private schools within walking distance to choose from. I needed to keep him at a school close enough that my little sister and brother could pick him up after they got out of school if I needed them to. By second grade, he transferred to Most Holy Name, a catholic school. St. Paul was merging with another Lutheran school that would have been out of the way for anyone to pick him up.

I look back from time to time and reflect on his first day of kindergarten. I can still see him with his little backpack, taking his time to go in the door, as most little boys do. I could see a bundle of fear and excitement as he took his first big step onto the pathway of his life's journey. His personality was in position; now it would take shape as he grew into the different stages of life. He would be with other kids, some with different characteristics and some with similar personalities. Times were soon to come where others would make him laugh or make him cry. He would learn to think and make little decisions on how to share, when to not share, who and what he liked and did not like. He would soon learn what he was good at doing and make choices from the opportunities that came his way.

It remained evident that he had an outgoing personality and was very protective of me, as only a son could be. He moved from being placed in a high chair to a pumpkin seat to sitting right in the front seat of the car. This is where he would park his pint-size body when he rode in the car with me. I would hold him in my right arm. There were no child seat belt laws or car seats. My son would not allow anyone to ride in the front seat of the car unless it was my mother. Fatman was protective of both me and my sister. She looked and acted far younger than her age. Fatman did not want anyone talking to her, even as a little fellow. My sister would take him to the skating rink with her all the time. She really loved to skate and loved outdoor activities as well. One Saturday, she had taken Fatman with her, and they were having a great time. Fatman was fine with other guys skating around them, but not when they would get too close to Necie. One young man, in particular, was skating next to the both of them and kept hitting on my sister. I guess the young fellow had gotten too close for comfort. Necie looked up, and Fatman bumped right into the boy because he didn't want him to talk to her. Fatman made it known that he had no desire to share his aunt with anyone.

When Fatman was about five or six, he wanted to see the new *Star Wars* movie. All the children wanted to see it. I had gotten tickets for us to attend the matinee at Halls Ferry Cinema Theatre. The day I had planned for us to go, he had his little mind made up that he was not going to pick up his toys. He was having an "I will do what I want" moment that day. Repeatedly, I told him to gather up his toys and put them away before we headed out to the movies. He blatantly refused to do so; after some time had gone by, I made it clear we were not going to the movies, and this would be his punishment for not following my instructions. His little heart was broken; you would have thought that I had done something really terrible to him. He boo-hooed and cried up a storm because he wanted to see *The Empire Strikes Back* with a child's passion. Fatman had every one of the toys from the previous *Star Wars* movie, and he treasured them. Eventually, he cried himself to sleep. It was getting close to three o'clock in the afternoon, and I had tickets for the five o'clock matinee. I woke him up and gave him his bath and told him we were going over to a friend's house to visit. He was unaware we were actually going to the movie, so he was still totally hurt and disappointed that he was not going to the show. He cried some more until he once again cried himself to sleep while riding in the car. About twenty-five minutes later, we arrived at the theatre parking lot, and it took a minute to find a good parking space. I called his name to awaken him after I parked and told him it was time to get out of the car. He did not want to get out and started crying again, but boy, oh boy, once he opened those little brown eyes, he totally stole my heart. His eyes lit up like fireworks with nothing less than joy and amazement when he saw we were at the movie and he was going to see *The Empire Strikes Back*. He grabbed me by the waist, hugging me so tightly. He had the biggest smile in the world on his face. Without closing my eyes, I can still visualize that smile. It was like he had just woken up on Christmas morning. As parents, we can almost touch the joy when our children are happy like that. It's the feeling a mother can only get from her child, and it tells her, "Mom, you did good!"

*****

Because of the forty-five-minute drive from my job in Chesterfield to Fatman's school, I was almost late for his kindergarten graduation. As usual, my mother was there, standing in the gap for her daughter, and so were my little sister and brother. I could always depend on them when it came to my son as well as if I needed anything. Fatman thrived in first grade, which was fun for him. He loved to read, which he was doing at a second-grade level, and really loved to write. My baby soon fell for his first love—no, not one of his classmates, but his first-grade teacher. He was the teacher's pet. Shoot, with his good manners and smarts, everybody loved my son. As Christmas break approached, he constantly bothered me about getting his teacher a gift. He had noticed that she wore neck scarfs all the time, so he requested I buy a scarf for her Christmas gift. I honored his wishes and purchased her a beautiful navy and green scarf. He was elated to give her his gift, and she enjoyed it. It was probably the most thoughtful gift she had received from one of her first graders.

Fatman played all types of sports, such as football and basketball, well. Family members always attended his games. My mother, who made it to every game, spent most of her time standing on the grass with the rest of us. Due to my work hours and getting through rush hour traffic, I would miss half of most of his games, but my family made sure he wasn't alone. He loved biking and break dancing and was excellent at both. Fatman could do tricks on his bike that you had to see to believe. The white house next door to us had caught fire and burned completely to the ground. Fatman took panels of wood and built a high ramp on the vacant lot where the house had burned down. He could go on that ramp and spin around like no other. I would be scared to death he was going to hurt himself and screaming at the top of my lungs for him to stop, but boys will always be boys. As soon as the parents turned their heads, the children would build another ramp and be riding on it again. When Fatman wanted a particular biking magazine, it took me forever to find it. I searched high and low until I found it while browsing through magazines at Dierberg's grocery store in Chesterfield. I had to get it for my baby. It did have a lot of good information in it about the rules of biking and the type of dirt bikes to buy. Since his birthday was a few weeks away, I kept the magazine and later surprised him with a real dirt bike and helmet. Since his birthday was in May, it was the right season for him to enjoy his gifts.

In the summers, we would throw his bike in the back seat of the car and head to Earle, Arkansas, like I had done as a kid. Most of our vacations were taken down south. My mother's mother and her sister, Aunt Effie D, lived in Earle. Both of my parents' folks had migrated from Mississippi to Arkansas. Earle was such a peaceful and free little town to be in. Everybody knew everybody, and your children were safe. Fatman could leave the house and bike around; as he passed by each corner, someone would holler or call my grandmother or my great-aunt Effie D to say they had seen him and what direction he was headed. Fatman also learned a little something about farming. Both my grandmother and Aunt Effie D raised chickens. When they let those baby chicks loose to run in the yard, Fatman would run around on his short legs trying to catch them, but he never did. It was a sight to see, and some of our happiest times together were spent in Earle.

My grandmother and Aunt Effie D would come to St. Louis during the winter months. My great-aunt was old, but she still had her wits about her. One evening, we left Fatman at home with Aunt Effie D. When we returned, we found them sitting at the kitchen table, and she had tears in her eyes. Fatman had told her a story about Jesus, which had touched her heart to no end. My great-aunt was the apple of my eye. Her enormous faith made her a strong Christian and someone I admired. She also believed in the words of the Bible with everything in her to let God, and not people, take vengeance. She was kind to everyone. She prayed and hummed hymns every day, and she took every opportunity to share her wisdom with us. To us, she was our grandmother. Fatman also received love and a little taste of wisdom from her. When vacation time was over, we would say our goodbyes, exchange hugs and kisses, and even shed a few tears.

*****

When Fatman was going into the sixth grade, the new school year would look a lot different than the previous years. Most Holy Name had thrown me a real curveball when it had announced it was going to close. We had just moved out of my mother's house and lived on McLaran on the northwestern side of the city. Decisions had to be made and fast; however, I wanted to make the best educational and economical decision for both of us. I had to lean more in the direction of his education because it was essential to me that he received the best schooling available. So I made the choice to enroll him in the Parkway School District. Parkway North was close to my job, making it accessible for me to get him in case of an emergency and to attend school meetings. The downside was that he would have to ride the school bus under the desegregation program. The most important thing was he would receive a quality education. In my resolve to send him to a public school, I didn't consider the different challenges of moving from a private school environment to a county/public school environment. Nor did I understand how the shift to unfamiliar territory would impact him on a personal and social level. It was a lateral move academically. However, St. Paul Lutheran School and Most Holy Name had both had a majority of African American students (although most of the teachers had been white). At Parkway North, the majority of the students were white and basically all of the teachers were white. This was his first opportunity to learn the differences in people and to identify who he was as a person. He had worn uniforms to school every day in the private school. Now he would have to adjust to wearing regular clothes in the public school and be prey to the different attitudes and statuses students associated with clothing. The playing field was no longer equal; school children judged each other on how they looked and how they dressed. This was a learning experience for both of us. Even though I dressed him well, the goal was not for him to outdress anyone else but for him to look nice and decent. Our children experience peer-to-peer challenges at all ages of life. It is an ongoing responsibility of a parent to learn and reexamine how we teach our children to deal with these challenges. Even when I was sick, I faithfully went to the school in my role as mother to make sure that my son was not mistreated and that he was doing the right things as a student to receive the educational base he needed.

Knocking on Heaven's Door

In November 1986, I was diagnosed with a brain aneurysm. That Sunday morning, I had a headache that wouldn't go away. The pain and throbbing had become so intense, it felt like a bomb was about to explode right inside my head. The headache would ease up for a short time, only to return even more intensified. No matter how much over-the-counter medication I took, it would not alleviate the pain. I had been treated for headaches since I was ten years old. My mother had taken me back and forth to the doctor because I always had a runny nose and headaches. After having my sinuses drained and flushed, I had been diagnosed with a severe sinus condition. I guess I grew out of the allergies, but at only twenty-nine years old, the headache had come back again; only this time, it would not go away. The pain, which originated on the right side of my head, hurt so badly. At the onset, I thought the headaches were triggered by the blurred vision I had been experiencing. However, my eyes had been examined recently, and my eyeglasses prescription was fairly new. On that Sunday, I had stayed in bed because the pain from the severe headache had caused me to sweat heavily. I was so hot and nauseated that I started to vomit. It had become one of the most unbearable pains. I had my son get my mother so she could call an ambulance. I was out of it by the time the ambulance had arrived. The emergency medical technicians rushed in, got me onto the stretcher, and worked on me on the ride to the hospital. My mother rode in the ambulance with me, and the rest of my family members followed the ambulance to Deaconess Hospital. The medical technicians wheeled me right into the emergency room and straight to an examination room, where doctors immediately began to work on me. Not long after the doctors finished, they sent me to get x-rays and consulted one another. The treatment plan for my horrendous migraine was a couple of prescriptions for pain along with a referral to see a neurologist. Absolutely nothing had been done to look for what had triggered such a gruesome headache. I was released to go home in basically the same condition I had arrived. The medicine the doctors had prescribed did nothing to stop the agony; I was in misery all night. Experiencing relentless pain, I went back to the emergency room the next morning.

This time I went to another hospital, Central Medical Center (CMC), close to my home. A friend of one of my brothers had a sister who was a registered nurse at CMC, and she had recommended I seek treatment there. I was in such distress at the time, I would have tried any hospital to stop the torture from this headache. The doctors there ordered more x-rays; however, the film results came back negative again. I was given a stronger prescription and sent home a second time. I went back to CMC the next day. This time the doctors told me I had a severe sinus infection. The doctor ordered an injection of Benadryl, and then I was sent out the door again. I was still experiencing a throbbing headache and could barely make it out of bed on Wednesday. I went back on Thursday and finally was admitted into the hospital. I underwent a series of x-rays and computerized tomography (CT) scans in which different views of my head were taken. They did a test called a "brain wave". The brain wave revealed a form of abnormality in my brain, but it was not clear what type of irregularity. They were simply going to treat me for the migraine headaches.

What happened to me at this point was totally bizarre. I was in a semiprivate room, and the day before I was to be released from the hospital, a new patient came into the room with me early that morning. She was an elderly lady. The nurse was not nice to her and began to mistreat her. I didn't like the way the nurse treated her. I immediately said something to the nurse. My roommate thanked me afterward. After a long week and a half of going from one hospital to the next and feeling like I was going to die at any minute from this horrible pain, I needed to do something to feel better. As a woman, we are vain in many different ways and sometimes at the most inopportune moments; I wanted to shampoo my hair, but an inner voice told me not to. My sister Necie would visit me every day, sometimes two or three times a day. I asked her to French braid my hair; I refused to have my head look bad regardless of my situation. She had to French braid my hair with me lying on my side, the pain was so dreadful. I had begun to feel very ill, with minimal strength left. It seemed like death was hovering over me, just waiting to come and take me away. After Necie finished my hair, she left and told me she would be back later on that evening. My mother, family, and friends took turns checking on me at the hospital throughout the day.

Later that day, my roommate's son came to visit her. I recognized him as a former schoolmate. God is amazing, placing his angels in our paths. His mother started telling him about the way the nurse had treated her and how I had spoken up to protect her. He was very grateful. Within thirty minutes, the headache resurfaced with a vengeance. The pain caused me to go in and out of consciousness. My roommate's son called for the nurse. She came quickly and contacted the doctor. The doctor arrived to check me over. I remember grabbing his lab coat as he was walking away and telling him that I couldn't see. He still marched out of the room as if he hadn't heard a doggone thing I had said. Shortly afterward, the nurse came back in and gave me a shot of Demerol for the pain. When Necie arrived a little while later, my roommate's son informed her of how the doctor had brushed off my comment about not being able to see. I came to just long enough to tell her that I still couldn't see. God was still doing his thing, but we had no clue. Necie immediately went and got the doctor. We felt my time here on earth was slowly running out, but God knew differently. The treating physician, puzzled by my loss of vision, called in an ophthalmologist, Garey L. Watkins, M.D., to examine me. As soon as he looked into my eyes, Dr. Watkins saw the vision loss had been caused by bleeding of a blood vessel—a leak somewhere in my brain. Dr. Watkins had them rush me to St. Louis University (SLU) Hospital and told my sister to call the rest of my family because I was bleeding in the brain and might not make it. He even rode with me in the ambulance to the other hospital.

It was scary to think that if I would have shampooed my hair, it could have caused my death. The doctors said I had gone into a semicoma. My mother got to the hospital as fast as she could. She had to make a decision—a decision that would determine if I would live or die. The doctors did not know how long I had been bleeding and could not discern if they would be able to stop the bleeding in time. The doctors wanted to do an angiogram test to confirm the origin of the bleeding. I would have to remain completely still during the test as any movement could cause me to become paralyzed or die. On the other hand, if I didn't have the angiogram, I could also die. I thank God for my momma and her motherly instincts because she agreed to me having the angiogram. It was a long wait for the test results for my mother and the rest of my family, especially my son. At only 13 years old, he was too young to completely understand, but he knew something was seriously wrong with his mother. Based on the outcome of the test, the doctors were able to determine where the bleeding was coming from and stabilize me for surgery the next morning. Not knowing if I would live or die must have felt like doomsday for my mother. However, as a God-fearing woman, she had faith like you could never know.

The next morning before surgery, my mother, sister, and son came to see me. I regained consciousness long enough to tell my sister and my son that I loved them, but I broke when it came time to tell my mother I loved her. The nurses asked them to leave the room because it was time for me to go and they wanted to keep me as calm as possible before my surgery. My last prayer before going to surgery was for God to let me live long enough to finish raising my son. I was told the surgery would take about six hours. The surgeon successfully repaired the aneurysm. When the surgeon, Dr. Del Coronado, came out to give my mother the good news of God's grace and mercy, she was so relieved that blood gushed from her nose. She had held onto so much love, fear, hope, and concern that she was overwhelmed with joy to learn that her baby had made it through surgery. There is nothing in this world or ever will be like that of a mother's love for her child. But I was not out of the woods just yet. The doctor advised that there was a seventy-two-hour time frame in which the brain could start to swell or bleed again. I vaguely remember them taking me from the recovery room to my room. I heard a voice shout, "That's my sister!" It had come from Pookie Boy. When he came to my bedside, I spoke my first words: "I made it, didn't I?" It was a statement and a question. Pookie Boy couldn't wait to tell the others that the first thing they knew was working was my mouth.

When I regained consciousness, I was able to tell the doctors and nurses that I could not see and that moving the lower part of my body was causing me excruciating pain. The nurses paged my neurosurgeon and the other doctors to come uncover what was causing these symptoms. After another round of testing, the team of doctors determined that I had blood in my spinal fluid. I endured three spinal taps spaced out over that week to relieve the pressure. Thank God that after the last spinal tap, the blood had dissipated enough to return my spinal fluid to its normal state. I was in unbelievable agony from the brain surgery and the subsequent needles being placed in my spinal cord. The spinal taps triggered unbearable back pain and throbbing headaches, which served as a constant reminder of the headache that had sent me to the hospital in the first place.

After another round of tests, the doctors' theory was that because my brain bled for an undetermined amount of time, the blood was able to seep out through a pin hole, filling the vitreous fluid behind my eyes. The extreme leakage of blood in my brain had caused my vision loss. There was a need for another surgery, a vitrectomy, to remove most of the blood in the fluid packs behind my eyes. However, the doctors decided the vitrectomy surgery would be too risky to carry out. The surgery itself could produce new bleeding. With no guarantee that the surgery would work and an increased concern of infection, not one doctor on the team was willing to take on that type of risk. All that was left to do was pray and to sleep in a reclined bed or chair with my head elevated in order to help move the residual blood back into my bloodstream. Only God and time would tell, so we let Mother Nature run its course.

Endless Love

I was in the hospital a few more weeks. I endured painful physical therapy done by an emotionless, nonempathetic therapist. I was able to stand up only to a certain degree, and my walk was wobbly. With my equilibrium off, I felt I had no balance at all. It was hard to start life over, regaining my balance and learning simple movement again. Although I had a long road of recovery, I had God on my side and the love of my son, my mother, my dear sister Necie, my brothers, extended family, and true friends.

My mother purchased a recliner for me to sleep in. The recliner became my best friend. After the surgery, I was unable to lay flat without feeling like I had a concrete block for a head. The doctors informed me it would take anywhere from a minimum of one year up to ten years for the brain to heal. I could not see anyone or anything, could not feed myself, and could not bathe myself. Feeling out of sorts, I was confused why this had happened and what would be my next move. The life I had had for twenty-nine years before this had become so blurred and far away. Debbie was gone somewhere, and I desperately wanted her back. My sister said I wasn't twenty-nine years old anymore but that my life had started over. I would not celebrate the age of thirty at my next birthday; I would have to start from the age of one year old and take it from there. God had given me a second chance at life.

My sister took off work an entire year to take care of me. Who does this? No one will ever need to tell me about the love of family. There was and is no way I could ever repay her. She sacrificed her present and future for me. Not only that, but I wasn't a good patient by a long shot. If I had had to have a caretaker back then, they probably would have physically abused me, God forbid. Only love or a person with the heart of God could deal with me. There were times when I would get irritated and throw glasses on the floor or at the wall. I would use all of the little strength I had, augmented by the anger inside me, to throw those glasses. Necie would wait until I had calmed down. It was a struggle, but eventually, I would make my way to my bedroom as I held onto the walls, taking one step at a time. Then I would sit down in my recliner, my friend. My sister, without a word, would come and sweep up the broken glass as if nothing had ever happened. She would make oatmeal or cream of wheat for breakfast and take her time helping me eat as I could not find my own mouth. Although I knew my mother loved me, she was not able to help me like Necie. She couldn't feed me because she couldn't look at me. It worried her to no end what I was going through and what was happening to me. They told me that my face had been so swollen that you could only see the tip of my nose, and one of my eyebrows was up higher toward the top of my head while the other was further down on my face. My head was half shaved. Surgery had saved my life but had taken its toll on my appearance. My brother Pookie Boy tried to convince me to shave my head and go to school to learn Braille so that I would be able to function and take care of myself. I did not know how, by what means, or when, but I was going to make it. If I had to live this way, I was going to live life to the fullest as I had always done.

After running my bath water, Necie would help me into the tub and help me bathe. Then she had to help me dress. She took me to all of my doctor's appointments. Lord, my sister had the patience of Job. My friend

Anita worked nights at a hospital, so she would come over and sit with me when she got off work every morning. This gave my sister time to run errands and get some rest. Everyone pitched in to help. I received prayers, flowers, fruit, food, and money for more than a year from so many people. God was good to me; it is true that you do reap what you sow. I had been good to a lot of people, and my goodness and love had come from my heart. Before this episode in my life, I had been the happiest person in the world. I was determined to get back to that life; Debbie was somewhere inside me trying to get out.

I followed up with Dr. Watkins regarding my vision as I had been classified as legally blind. Dr. Watkins told me I needed to meet with a retinal specialist and referred me to one in Clayton, Missouri. This new doctor was amazing and very kind. On my first visit with him, we talked about my vision and discussed the thread of events that had occurred from the time of my first headaches. He prayed before he did the examination. After the examination, he told me that I may never see again. It would take time for the swelling from the brain surgery to go down; however, once the swelling went down, the blood could start draining back into my system and hopefully I would regain some vision. He wasn't going to give up on me. I thank God I had the job I did back then. I went on disability, and my employer continued my insurance, which covered my medical bills for eighteen months. My family was extraordinary, taking care of both me and my son. They never missed a beat in our needs, wants, or desires being met. Now this reminded me of the prayer, "Footprints"; Jesus had been carrying me, and I didn't even know it.

Recovery was slow and painful. My vision came back slowly and in an unusual manner. My peripheral vision came back first. I could not make out the images at first. Whatever and whomever I saw were frightening because the graphics were magnified. If a regular loaf of bread was in front of me, it would look like a humongous dark figure with light movement. I had nothing solid to grab hold of in my new world. Details remained elusive and felt unreal. I had so many questions. What was happening to me? Would I see again? Would I be able to see my son grow up? Would I ever see my mother's face again? It was a scary point in my life, but I kept praying, fighting, and pushing myself.

I have always heard that if you lose use of a limb, the body compensates somehow and makes the other limb stronger. I believe it as fact. With the loss of my vision, my other senses became stronger. My little brother Kenneth said, "You hear like a German shepherd and smell like a Doberman pinscher." This is when I learned how to depend on my instincts and developed into an authentic Pisces, led by my spirit and gut feeling. Logic no longer had a place in my life since nothing made sense. But there were positives, too. I made the discovery during my recuperation that I couldn't judge a book by its cover without my sense of sight. Being incompetent to prejudge anyone totally rocked my world. All my other senses had taken on new dimensions. I had to make a choice: drown in self-pity or embrace life with what I had, which was all I had. With a long recovery ahead of me, I became a healing work in progress.

It had started out as a dark winding road for me and my son. My son was my reason for getting up every morning and making it through each day. It was truly hard on him having to watch how I had deteriorated and had become unable to personally care for the both of us. We were unable to spend mother and son time together because I had no energy. All I could do at the beginning of my rehabilitation was take medication, eat what my stomach could keep down, and sleep. The pain medication left me nauseated, and it took time for me to build up the energy to be able to sit up for long periods of time. Also, my lower back was still sore from the spinal taps I had endured. I won't ever know the profound adverse effect this had on my son. Nor will I ever know the hurt, the powerless feelings, and thoughts he had as he watched me day in and day out. Did he see me getting better, or could he only see a state of no return? He had my mother, sister, and brother, but who did he really turn to when he needed to talk?

Would he turn to a stranger, someone who would lead him astray … away from me … away from the tribulations he had grown accustomed to?

The holidays were fast approaching. Christmas was right around the corner, and Santa would be getting on his sleigh to deliver joy all over the world. I had had a premonition that something was going to happen to me before the holidays, so I had gotten most of my Christmas shopping done in October. This was the first time in my life I had finished shopping for the holidays in October or November. I had gotten my son a weight set, which was hidden under my bed. He had clothes, board games, and, of course, new tennis shoes and boots. God speaks to us in many ways; he had guided me to get ready for this holiday early because he knew I would not be able to do anything in December. God had also given warning to my father and my great uncle Wick before their deaths. They knew their time on earth was short, so they made sure their wives and families would be ok. Yes, we may be sent signs, but it is up to us to notice them and obey him. In my living room, I had a black and gold étagère that was shaped in a big diamond with glass shelving. We used the étagère as our Christmas tree, with the gifts piled up under the bottom shelf, on the sides of the étagère, and stacked up in front of it. I couldn't see it, but everyone told me how beautiful it was and took pictures so that I would be able to see it when my vision returned. Christmas was bittersweet that year for my family. My son had his mother, my mother had her daughter, and my brothers and sister had their sister, but they only had part of her. My face and head were still swollen, so it was hard for them to look at me. My two nieces came over to get their gifts; however, they would not come near me because of the way I looked. One thing is for sure, I did not look like their aunt. Not one person in the family took a photo of me so that I could see myself later.

I can recall the time Necie had run my bath water and went to get something from my mother's house next door. By the time she had returned, I had made it over and into the tub all by myself. Talk about being happy, boy I was ready. Bit by bit, I became strong enough and in enough control to begin feeding myself. I was coming back to life! Slowly, I got my balance back and was able to dress myself. Although I didn't always get the clothes on the right side out or the buttons aligned with the correct button holes, the point was I got the clothes on by myself.

My mother would come over daily to sit with me. Our conversations were different now; she was faced with looking at her baby girl struggling to regain her strength and her sight, not to mention fighting to get her life back. I could always hear the quiver in her voice as she held back the tears to be strong for the both of us. God gives us that special gift to hold up under any circumstance when it comes to our children.

I had a passion for music and dancing. As my balance was still off, I could listen to music but not dance. One day, the radio was playing one of Luther Vandross's songs, and it sounded so good to me. I could not shake, twist, or turn, but the music was in me and I wanted to get up and dance so badly. As the song continued to play, I had a burning desire to see if I could just stand up in a pair of high heels. If I could stand for a second or two, it would mean that I was one step closer in my healing process and one step closer to the dance floor. I asked my mother to get a pair of my heels out of the closet for me. I could feel her hesitancy as she questioned me why. I told her I wanted to see if my shoes still fit, and if they did, I wanted to try to stand up, with her help, of course. She agreed and got me a pair. My mother helped me put each shoe on; they felt pretty good. The challenge now was for me to stand up in them. My mother grabbed me by my left side and held me close to her as I started to rise up from the recliner. A few seconds later, I was almost straight. After a deep breath and a silent prayer, I straightened my knees and back more. Unbelievably, I was standing in my high heels with her holding me. She took me a few short steps down the hallway, still holding tight to her little girl as she always had done to make sure I didn't fall. I wanted to find out how long I could stand up with my shoes on by myself. The music was still playing and moving within me. Music has a way of doing strange and beautiful things to you. It can spark a tear of joy and in the next note spark a tear of pain. Music can make you want to run, jump, shout, or give you the craving to stand up in your high-heeled shoes. The feeling hit like a flash of light as the lyrics went deeper into my soul. I threw one hand up in the air and started to lightly twist from side to side and down, or as close as I could toward the floor, while my mother's grip got even tighter. In slow motion, I started to rise back up again, with a wobble or two. This was my sign—the feeling of life in the small movement of dance and the ability to stand up in my chocolate brown high heels. I couldn't move another step, so my mother had to help me out of the shoes and get me back to my chair. But I was filled with joy, knowing I had taken a small step in returning to the life of Debbie.

Out of the Blue

It had only been a few months since my son and I had moved to North County before the loneliness and longing for my life back had started to overcome me. I wanted someone to save both me and my son. Life started moving at a faster pace as I recovered. Although I had made a lot of progress, I was still so far behind. In the spring of 1990, I was hanging out in my brother's confectionary store when this tall man came in to buy a Snickers candy bar. My cousin Connie, my friend Linda, and my two nieces were there as well. I could see well enough to know he was a good-looking hunk of a man. Somehow, we built an entire conversation around a candy bar. We introduced ourselves, and he told us his name was Sabastian. He called me the next day, and from then, our hearts started to beat for each other. It was both a physical and an emotional attraction. The sound of Sabastian's voice could rock my world. We both fell madly in love, and there was no stopping us as we moved quickly through a courtship. After six months, he asked my mother for my hand in marriage on Labor Day. My mother responded, "The both of you will get married, but how long will it last?" He got permission from my brothers as well. With Pookie Boy and Ken's approval, we planned a wedding in less than six months. My family paid for my wedding, a beautiful one, even though they had reservations about me marrying him. There was something about him that wasn't right, but no one could put their finger on it. Even my son had his reservations. But, you know, I was in love, stubborn, and no one could convince me not to get married. It goes back to the saying, "You make your bed hard, and you lie in it." My family loved me enough to let me go through with the wedding, knowing that they would be there when the rubber hit the road in our marriage, which it eventually did. At first, he gave me everything in the world—diamonds, pearls, clothes—and took care of all the household bills. He covered me with love and romance and showered me with gifts. He protected me from everyone. We had been married just over a year when, out of the blue, tragedy took a hold of my family's life.

It was ten on a Wednesday morning when the telephone rang. A man on the other end of the phone asked, "Are you GDevonte's mother?" I replied, "Yes, I am his mother." The man, who was an officer, told me that I needed to come to the hospital right away; my son had been injured and was in the intensive care unit. At that moment, time stopped. The inside of my stomach balled up into knots, and fear overcame me in an instant. My husband asked, "What's wrong?" While screaming and crying, I said, "Fatman is in the hospital. I have to go right now and see what has happened to my baby, got to leave right now!" I dressed in whatever I could find while thinking, "Will my baby be alright?" My son had a son who was only six weeks old. His girlfriend had been almost eight months' pregnant when I found out he was going to be a father. I had been so excited when GDevonte Jr. was born. Fatman kept the baby at our house most of the time. It was pure joy to see him bathe and feed his son. I had taken a lot of photos of them, and my favorite one showed him asleep with GDevonte Jr. in his arms as if he were protecting him from the entire world.

So after the terrifying phone call, a voice within me told me to get his girlfriend and his son. They needed to be there; Fatman needed his son with him. I don't care who you are or where you are in life, when trouble comes, you need the ones you love and who love you by your side.

We left the house immediately and picked up his girlfriend and his son. They lived right by the hospital. When we arrived at the hospital, a police officer told us that Fatman had been hit in the head with a blunt object. The doctor said, "He had a severe cerebral trauma to the brain. We had to perform an emergency brain surgery to release the pressure in order to stop the swelling." My eighteen-year-old baby was in a coma. This could not be happening to us. This was not real, not now, not ever. A sickness came up from my stomach into my chest; I felt like it was choking me. I just screamed, "No, no, not Fatman!" I started to think and believe that it was not happening. How could this be possible, for my own child to leave this earth before me? The shock of that possibility sent me into an unnatural state. I became overwhelmed with numbness, confusion, and disorientation. The light of life within me had begun to die out. When I saw him, there were no words in the dictionary to explain the horror of seeing my child lying lifeless on a ventilator with nurses and machines surrounding his bed. I don't even know if I knew if God was there. It's not like I had given up on my faith. But it was only me and Fatman at this moment. Everyone else was invisible, except for the person who did this. Fatman could not tell me who had hurt him, and all I could think about was who had done this to my child and why couldn't I have been there.

As I looked on, I thought about the last time I had seen my son. I had fried some jack salmon fish and made macaroni and cheese. Fatman wanted to go somewhere he should not have been going. I had made several attempts to get him to stay home and have dinner with us. Although he had called a cab to come pick him up, he wasn't about to leave the food behind. He had grabbed some aluminum foil and got some fish and macaroni and cheese. Fatman loved his momma's mac and cheese.

While waiting for his taxi to come, I could see that he was uneasy about something, which didn't sit well with my spirit. It actually made me very afraid. We had continued to talk as he shoved food down his throat, as boys do when they have somewhere to be. Eat and run. I had tickets to see the Globetrotters show that day. It would be my first time going, even though Fatman had seen them before. I had always gotten tickets for him to go with my sister and brother because all three of them truly loved basketball. My husband had gotten these tickets, but he had to work. I had extended an invitation to a friend to go with me. I had said to my son, "This is going to be the first time I'm seeing the Globetrotters play." He responded, "It's a first time for everything, ain't it, momma?" I had told him, "Yes, you live long enough, you will always have a first."

Suddenly, there had been a knock on the door. Fatman had jumped in a panic. His spirit jumped and so did mine. I saw terror or something all over my son. I pleaded for him to stay, but he was moving too fast and left anyway. Immediately, I had started to pray to God to keep him safe from harm. I had already committed to going with a friend to the show, so I went. I could not tell you what had happened during the game because the entire time I was thinking of my child and praying.

I had been there every time he had called, and even when he didn't call, I would show up. We know when things aren't right with our children, but we don't know when, how, or where trouble will take place. A mother's spirit and instinct will haunt us to the end. You have uneasy feelings and fears, and you see things in your child, things they see and feel that no one else can perceive. When trouble is in their path, they become restless spirits; there is something in their eyes, their words, or just their mannerisms that tell you something is not quite right. It tears away at your being every day; it grows a root deep in your heart and gut that cannot be cut away. They may cut the umbilical cord after birth, but it doesn't sever the connection between a mother and her child. It is a bond for life, and it will continue on after death. God always forewarns us. The old folks called them warning signs. Our children receive those same signs, but it is up to them to take heed. I am not sure at his level of understanding if Fatman recognized these warning signs, and if he did, how many signs he had received. I began to struggle with thoughts that something was going to happen to my baby. There was some type of veil over him that I could not break through. He was only eighteen and one-half, and his son, GDevonte Jr., was less than two months old. I thought back to when I was pregnant with him, and it triggered a memory of the girl I had known who was pregnant at the same time as me but delivered her baby before I did. She had died during the C-section delivery, but they were able to save her child. Now my son's child was facing the prospect of growing up without a father like that baby grew up without a mother.

Now my son had come to the life-or-death fork in the road. How could my grandson grow up without his father? Watching him in his hospital room of the intensive care unit, oh God, it hurt so badly, and I was so afraid. When I saw him on the breathing machine—not able to see me, talk to me, and only God knows if he could hear me—the light of faith and hope started to dim rapidly. I held his hand in mine and laid my face on his heart. Tears running down my face, I cried, "Fatman, Fatman, can you hear me? Fatman, everything is going to be alright. Baby, don't give up; you can beat this. Fatman, please, can you hear me?" I was hoping and praying that I wasn't too late. My husband tried to talk to him. My family, loved ones, friends, and his friends were all in the waiting room. I was living a nightmare. This had come to be a fight of faith, a fight for life, and our fight against death. My son had been robbed and hit in the head with a crowbar. With his ID gone, the police had been unable to identify him, so he was fingerprinted sometime after his surgery. My son had been alone when he underwent the knife. Had the surgeon even cared about him? Had they given him the best care, or was he just another black child who had arrived at the hospital and they did what was needed to fill the requirements of an emergency room trauma? Did they even care he was my son, not a hoodlum, not a murderer, not an ex-con, not a rapist nor a robber, a child just like theirs with a mother who needed for them to do everything in their power to save his life? I will never, ever know if the staff had exhausted all of their medical options to prevent his death.

God had heard and answered my prayer to leave me here to raise my son. He knew how much I loved my baby, but now he was taking him away from me. Losing a child is the most devastating, heartbreaking thing that could ever happen to anyone. Healing is a long, painful, and lonely journey, a process with no road map to follow. You never get over it, but you learn how to live again. There is no putting the pieces back into the puzzle. A physical piece is missing but alive in your heart and mind because every moment from the time of conception has been spent preparing for your child's future.

You know, when God made man, he breathed the breath of life into him. My son's, my only child's, life had ended … no, it had been taken from him, and he had taken his last breath of life only to exhale the breath of death. My son was not going home with me this time. The Lord had prepared a place for him, and I had to prepare a final resting place for my baby. I had to have his body moved from the hospital to the funeral home. We were in the middle of nowhere. I could hardly breathe in and out. There were no more words. My last words to him had been, "I love you, Fatman." I love you was all I could say. I could not hold him anymore; we'd had our final hug. No more cuddles, no more jumping up and down in my bed, no more phone calls, no more hearing his voice say, "Momma." I stayed in his hospital room as long as I could because once you leave, there is no going back, no turning around, and nowhere left to go.

A funeral is an occasion set aside for mourning, paying the last respects, and reading the eulogy. All I knew was that I wanted the best for my baby in his journey home just as I had wanted the best for his life. I was only physically at the funeral; my mind and spirit were in another dimension. I had him placed in a vault where his body would be sealed and he would remain as my physical son for twenty-five years. Yes, as his mother, I still felt obligated to protect my baby; the love of one's child never ends. After the funeral was over, a period had come where I had to face reality alone. Kind words, hugs, kisses, prayers, people telling you it will be alright ... you are unable to feel, see, or hear what they are saying or doing. There was no reason to smile, laugh, or have other people in your life. The death of your child brings many losses to grieve. I not only lost the physical presence of my child, but also all of the dreams, hopes, and aspirations I had for him as well as his own hopes and ambitions. The joys and challenges of raising him were now only a memory. It seemed unreal that my child was gone. The sudden loss raised a host of other feelings. On top of the deep pain and sadness, the emotional detachment caused me to become severely depressed. I had a sense that no one could help me. They had not suffered a loss like I had, so what do they know? I had lost my only child when he was a fresh-faced teenager. He had not even begun to live, let alone understand his life or life in general. Losing him caused me unbearable feelings of grief, guilt, and anger. I isolated myself from everyone and everything. No longer did I have anything in common with life. I became emotionally paralyzed.

Like other bereaved parents, I carry feelings of guilt as if I could have prevented it from happening. I had become the judge and jury, only to be found guilty as charged. *I should have been there, it should have been me, why my child,* played over and over in my mind. As a mother, I regretted failing to have done something to prevent his death. I felt that I should have had more control over his life and the ability to keep him out of harm's way, but I was his mother and not God. With my child gone, I felt like I had miscarried at life. I no longer shared a bond with humanity. How could I justify or validate who I was when my child was gone and no one could identify with me? I did not want the pity of others. The thoughts and notions of others feeling sorry for me bombarded me. *Please don't feel sorry for me,* I thought, *because I can handle this all by myself.*

So many things were left unfinished: things not said, not done, or things I know could have been reconciled. By the time your children reach young adulthood, their lives have expanded beyond the sphere of their home. They have developed a circle of friends, acquaintances, and adults through school, sports, jobs, hobbies, church, dating, and the vast number of other activities they have been involved in. Everyone is touched by the passing of a child; removing one person from the fabric of this world leaves a gap. I found myself in search of and looking for my teenager. There were instances when I saw people who resembled him, who walked like he did, and at times, I would believe it *was* him. When you lose a child, you discover yourself looking for your child to come home, as I did over and over again. It was a never-ending, vicious cycle. I could hear his laughter, see his smile on his face, but slowly the images start to fade away.

I wanted answers to why this had to happen. Hurt and angry for many years, I couldn't see the glass half full or half empty—for me, there was no glass at all. Money or material things had no value; physical things could not replace his life. I had to stand in the gap for Fatman and raise his son, even though I was still grieving for his father. The strange thing is that I loved my grandson with a goal … a goal and a vow: no one would harm or hurt him. It was a fight within me where no other fight existed, a love that I gave unknowingly, and a joy that I could not share with others.

People will always ask the age-old questions, "Do you have any children?" or "How old are your kids?" as a way to connect with you. I responded with all types of answers. Sometimes I would say no, and to strangers, I would answer with a yes and then find myself crying and trying to explain it at the same time. For the most part, people don't actually care how you feel; people only wanted to know the details of what had happened. Before my mother passed away, she tried to teach me how to answer that question. She told me to say, "Yes, I have a son, and he passed away," and then put an end to the subject. It was not that simple for me to put a period at the end of that sentence. Once I would say that he had passed away, someone would ask, "When, how old was he, what happened?" when those persons didn't even know me. I continued to grow stronger or angrier—I still don't know which one it was—so I started to answer, "My son passed away, but I have a grandson." This is when I realized that I was validating his death and who I was with the use of the conjunction "but". I had moved to the next phase of healing, or so I thought. Then if someone asked what had happened, I would let them know that I didn't want to talk about. However, people would become angry that I didn't give them additional information on my child's death, and some would look at me as if *I* had a problem. No, they were the ones with the problem. What right did they have to know the details of my pain? What had they suffered in their life?

Eventually, I learned how to say that I had a son and he is deceased with a period at the end of the statement. I didn't owe any explanations to anyone, and people did not have the right to be so inconsiderate. There is etiquette to be followed when a person has lost a loved one, especially a child.

It was hard to see the light at the end of the tunnel beyond all the pain, hurt, controversy, and denial. The questions of why continued to play in my head over again. Yes, it will get better in time; however, there will always be points in your life when you relive your season of loss as if it were happening right then. No one could comprehend the emotional roller coaster ride I took. I had to figure out who I was, where I belonged, and if I still deserved to be happy.

*****

Holidays will remain as holidays; Thanksgiving Day and Christmas are for family and friends, and birthdays remain important, especially those of your children. When I celebrate my grandson's birthday, I celebrate the birth of his life and his accomplishments; at the same time, I celebrate the life of his father, my son, and mourn his death. No matter what, with the celebration comes the reality that his father is not with us anymore. I lost a son, his son lost a father, and this is not the natural order. A family will always struggle with the loss of a child, a son, a daughter, a mother, a father, a sister, or a brother.

The loss of a child is a break in the entire family tree. Memories have to be kept sacred in order for the family to remain whole. This is where you discover how to fight the good fight of faith. If not, you too will die—not a physical death, but an emotional and spiritual death. If the memories fade away, the family will never heal.

I would go through periods in life when unanswered questions would consume my every thought. When I would read some of Fatman's writings, I toiled with the idea that he had been trying to tell me he was leaving me soon. One summer night in 1989, I had punished him by not letting him go outside since he did not turn in his homework. Fatman had wanted to go outside so badly, one would have thought it was a life-threatening event. He had been so upset until he typed up this letter late that night.

LIFE IS TOO HARD...................................

Life is full of games and you have to look for the ones who persude you and leads you into trouble , those are the ones who are likely get you into trouble. Some people look at life as one great big game and dont care about there self, and some people look at life at more serious perpective and tries to live life at it fullest and takes it day by day. Me personaly dont know. Cause life is so confusing and you dont know which road to take, so you have to be carefull in the decsion you make and be staight up with yourself and aknowledge the things around you. You always get trick by the ones you think is by yourside , you cant make up for the things you do you can only try to keep it from happening again. Learn to think realisticaly and come from the heart. You cant be the best in every thing you just have to make it work and make it worth the trouble you have to go through. Cause if you dont you are considerd a failure.There is all ways going to be a person who just spoils your day but in time you will have to look over that . I think Im bless cause so many people are tring to help me,then again there is someone who tries to bring you down with there hate.

Some times you think the world is agaist you but you create your own prombles and you have to find some way to deal with them.You try to be peacefull but someone out there allways brek that level of consitration cause they hate to see you walk with your head up in the most intesse situaion but they are only jealous and is is a sucker for reality . Reality is a hard word to define cause it is so many ways you can define it, every one has they own definiton of reality but you must learn to kick reality your own way.When your not a little boy and your faimily is gone your going to get lead the wrong way.But to me the greatest love of all comes from the love you have for your self and the love you obtain from the peoplEaround you.

Mothers and fathers who have lost their children think differently about one another as it relates to their losses. Folks treat you differently depending on how your children died. My son's life was taken, but I have met mothers who have lost their children via car accident, suicide, cancer, drug overdoses, and an array of medical illnesses. A separation derives from how your child left this earth. About fifteen years after Fatman's death, one of his friends was killed in a car accident. His friend's mother and I crossed paths at a dance class. We talked about our sons' lives and their deaths. It was a bitter, bittersweet moment. His mother introduced me to someone she knew, telling this person about our sons' friendship. She spoke about what great friends they had been and how they had passed away at different times; however, she separated their deaths by explaining that her son had died in a car accident, but my son had been killed. I don't know why this happens, but people seem to believe that the way a person dies makes a difference, as if the child whose life was not taken by the hands of another was better. Instead of judging, we should think about the hearts of others because we are all mothers and fathers who have lost one of the most precious gifts that God could ever give. During a stressful event such as death, we look for answers and ways to make the facts easier to accept so we can make it through that day or night. It is a coping mechanism, but we all deserve the opportunity to heal and find peace in our own ways. The only peace that I was able to grasp onto was that my son did not die in the streets.

When the day has ended and night has fallen, my baby is still gone. And each day that comes, I have to awaken without him. I had to find a way to keep going, to live, to look at people without crying, without worrying if they could see right through me. I needed to learn to deal with how people saw me or what I thought they saw in me.

I had to look into my mother's eyes and see the love and hurt she carried for me and herself. I watched her health deteriorate because she could not handle the loss of her grandchild, whom she had loved with all her heart and soul—the grandson raised in her house, her future, and the generation that would carry on her and her husband's legacy. When Fatman was a little baby, my mother would take the petroleum jelly or baby oil and put it all over his body, getting him just as shiny as she could. She would fry eggs and mash them up and feed them to him at three months old because she thought he was too small and needed to gain some weight. My mother had retired early, but she still had wanted to stay busy. She had taken a part-time job as a school bus monitor to keep the children on track while riding the bus to and from school. She had taken my son on the bus ride with her every day. He had called her the shoe lady because she would always buy him his shoes. Fatman would always ask her, "Mutt, can I have some of this, can I have some of that?" and she would give it to him every time. Every holiday, he had gotten new tennis shoes, boots, and dress shoes. But now there would be no more of him begging for candy or money, no more hugs and kisses. He would not be there to get her a BC or Stanback aspirin or rub her head with alcohol when she had a headache.

I also had to watch my little sister and brother try to make it through each day and my nieces and nephews search for answers because they were being asked the same questions I was. I had to see my big brother for the first time become speechless, not knowing what to say or do. He had always had the answers or could make it better for me in the past. Now I had to find a way to stop crying, to start laughing again, and to find a way through the tunnel of life. My sister said she would never love another child again. She fought so hard to push her great-nephew, GDevonte Jr., away, but he kept coming back into her heart. He kept coming back to all of us. My son Fatman had written a note to his son on the back of a picture of my mother, telling him how special his great-grandmother was. My sister discovered this photo and handwritten note a long time after my son had passed away.

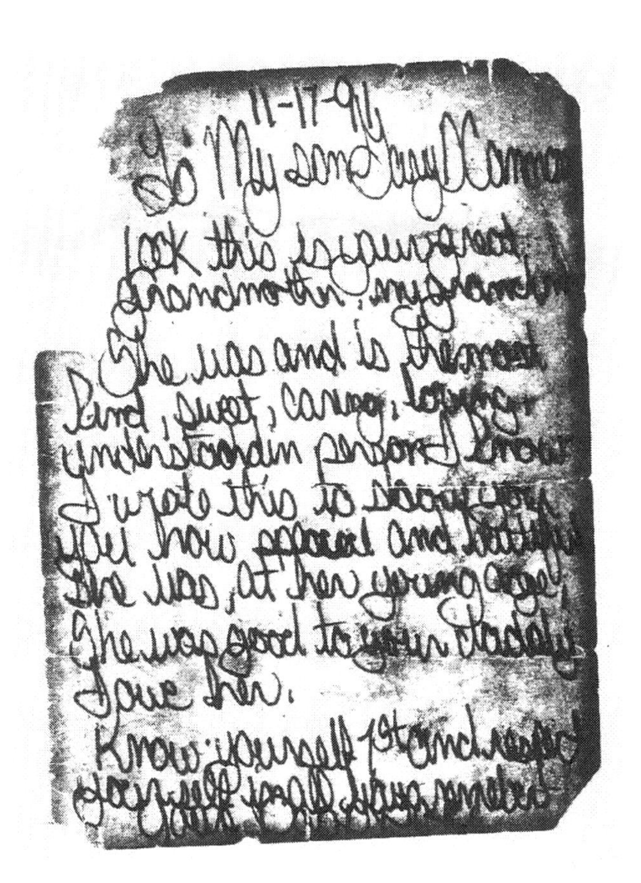

11-17-96

To My son Gary D Cannamore

Look this is your great
grandmother, my grandmother.
She was and is the most
kind, sweet, caring, loving,
understanding person I know.
I wrote this to show you
you how special and beautiful
she was, at her young age.
She was good to your daddy.
Love her.

Know yourself 1st and respect
yourself for all. Always remember

Midnight Through the Day

My weapons were filled with ammunition of pain, strong resentment, and bitterness from the betrayal of life. A negative driving force pierced the core of my heart, injecting venom into every thought. I lost my faith in God; how could he, the highest of all, let this happen to my child? Nothing happens by chance. There is a cause and effect behind all that happens, no matter how small or insignificant it appears to us. God established laws and timetables long before we were born.

I had lost all interest in life and people. I did not care what happened to me. It was painful for me to see other teenagers. I could not laugh or feel for other people and their problems. Their issues seemed trivial. They had their children; how could they possibly be unhappy? I hadn't gone back to work, so there wasn't any reason for me to go outside; there was no need for people in my life. I had lost a sense of purpose and couldn't see how life could be worth living. The loss of my child took everything from within me and left me deeply wounded spiritually. I blamed God for letting my only child die. The grief caused me unbearable pain and hatred. I had always loved music, but the songs were not for me anymore. When my son passed away, I had thrown out all the music from my house: out went the 45s and 33s. No more jazz, R&B, or love songs. The dance and music in me had gone along with my smile.

Along with grieving for my child, I was mourning the loss of a marriage. My husband had dishonored his vows to me. He had gotten another woman pregnant sometime before the death of my son. My mother had said, "He committed the ultimate crime." The only way for me to grieve and recover was to leave him and everything to do with the marriage behind.

On New Year's Eve, 1998, my grief had run its course, and it was time for something to change. Now single but not dating, I couldn't find anyone that I could be with so that I wouldn't have to be alone. My baby had passed away on the 14th of January, so I dreaded when each new year came in because I would relive his death. I called my brothers and friends, who all had dates that evening, and I was a mess. I was walking and crying when I just fell to my knees and cried out to God, "Please, please, Father, give me and my family peace with the death of my son." At that moment, without realizing it, I was establishing a new relationship with God. After the loss of a child, God will somehow, through his divine intervention, gut you all the way, rearrange you, and via the people around you and those who come into your life, turn you into you a new individual, piece by piece, moment by moment, spirit by spirit.

The old Debbie had been full of joyful laughter and had the biggest, radiant smile imaginable. In order to start healing, I had to be reincarnated into a new person with elements of the old me. I changed physically, mentally, emotionally as well as spiritually. It took well over two years before I could laugh like Debbie again. The laugh itself actually hurt when it first came out. I learned how to rechannel my anger into positive thoughts and recognize that the anger had been masking the pain. During my healing, I discovered that I would never be the same person I had been, but I didn't have to remain the angry person I had become. Healing is ongoing; you give a little of yourself away, you keep a little, and you hope for something even greater. I will always have to reinvent myself, be it through the questions embedded in my mind or by the mixture of joy and pain as the answers slowly reveal themselves. It is a constant reevaluation of my perception of life brought on by the loss of my only child, and it doesn't match or mirror anyone else's experience. Others will never understand that there was no middle for me; I was either too happy or too sad. God gave me periods of joy to counterbalance the substantial sadness, which kept me from losing my mind. This was and is my personal coping mechanism: I don't take life for granted. Not everyone gets a second chance like I did. My baby did not get a second chance. How you cope with the loss of a child is a reflection of who you are. It is a step-by-step and day-by-day process. There are no written rules on how to heal.

It seemed as if I were in between dreams, learning how to function as what society considered a "normal" person. I had to find a way to give back, give a part of me, and come up with an approach to help other children. I needed to visualize a course of action to help others as a pathway for me to heal. I had taken the realtor exam and passed it a year after my son had passed away and begun to sell real estate. My divorce had been finalized around the same time. I was angry, afraid, and lost, stuck in a bubble of my own making. The real estate broker had partnered me with a top agent, a wonderful woman named Scotland. She was about ten or twelve years older than I was, a very classy lady. Scotland reminded me of my mother. She was a great communicator and could read people pretty well. She partnered with me on my first listing appointment. I was in awe watching her in action, from her charm to her ability to negotiate. I wanted to emulate her character, so much of which was like my mother and also like who I used to be. It was like God had placed her in my life to help me move on; the Holy Spirit had provided me with the fortitude to keep the pain and remember who I used to be and how that person was still inside me. We eventually became good business friends. God moving me forward, he had begun placing people in my life to ensure that I did not falter.

Amazingly enough, out of all the properties I listed, only one did not sell. It wasn't like I was a top-listing agent, but I thought I was building a career that would take me to some sort of new life and a new "normal". Nevertheless, challenges still confronted me. Unbeknown to everyone else, I remained a totally dysfunctional real estate agent. My vision was off, I had to try to smile when dealing with prospective clients, and I listened to people talk about their children with the undisclosed fear that someone would ask me if I was married or if I had any children. I could deal with saying I was divorced, which was a no-brainer, but having to tell a stranger my child was gone was a whole other monster. I spent more time crying and grieving, just a pitiful person. The remnants of a defunct marriage hovered over me, like a dark cloud that debilitated my life. My clients never knew that I was on an emotional roller coaster. They thought I didn't care and didn't have their best interests at heart.

I didn't even know where my heart was. It was covered with pain and grief. Then there were those who thought I was a doormat and attempted to disrespect me or deceive me in the real estate business. One time, I was on telephone duty and taking calls for the office. A white male agent accused me of taking his call; standing over me, he went off on me. I did not know what to do. I wondered what else could happen to me. I cried and was humiliated. Anyone who knew me before I had lost my child knew that that would have never happened to me. He would have been the one crying. But there was no fight in me. My friend Scotland, again showing her grace, told me that day, "If anyone ever stands up while talking to you, you stand up. Never sit down and allow another person to speak to you in a condescending manner."

The embarrassment of this incident, the ups and downs of my marriage, and the grief were all too much, so I eventually left that sales office. I called Sigma Chemical Company where I had been employed long before my aneurysm and when my son had been alive. They rehired me right away. This was a place where I did not have to explain my loss or my love for my child. I did not have to find my way; they knew who I was.

While gaining security by working at Sigma, it was inevitable that I would transfer to another brokerage firm to continue with real estate part-time. As time passed, I found a small real estate office with new people. It was as if I had a place to hide, a simple place to discover where my place was in life. The agents were nice and helpful. The broker was professional and had done well with his business. During our initial meeting, I told the broker a little about myself with a beacon of hope that he could relate to me enough for us to have an open communication about my current situation.

Can you imagine showing property to people with families as well as to couples with hopes of having children and being in a place of life like I was, trying to find hope in a future for yourself? The broker partnered me with a female agent. He had given her a lot of business, and she had done well. In her mind, she was the top of the top. I went on a few listing appointments with her. On one of the appointments, she told me if I worked with her on the listing and moved this property, she would split the commission fifty-fifty. This was a win-win for me. Then my sister, who had always been such a blessing to me, gave me a lead on my first solo listing in the new office. I needed all the closings I could get because I was slowly working my way out from under the divorce. Preparation always meets opportunity. Enough had been taken from me: my son, my marriage. There was no more to be taken by anyone. This was my true mind-set; it lay beneath my half-smile, the hurt, and the pain. I was in a lonely place without my son, devoid of life. About six months had gone by since I had started working at the second brokerage firm. I was working a full-time job and part-time as an agent to cover all my bases in starting a new life.

God's grace continued to cover me. One rainy day, I was sitting in my car at a red light when a car hit me from behind. The driver had fallen asleep at the wheel. The impact knocked my car through the intersection and turned it in the opposite direction. I had just missed the oncoming traffic. I came to enough to dial 911 on my cell phone. The fire trucks arrived before the ambulance did. As they were asking me questions and removing me from the car, one of the firemen noticed the name of the real estate brokerage firm on my name tag. The owner of the company was a fireman as well, so, oh my goodness, did they take care of me and my car. I was so grateful to God for his mercy and how he continued to place angels in my path.

The real estate office sent flowers to my other job. I thought, *What a wonderful place to be.* The other agent and I were finally able to close a deal on a property, but the commission did not work out as agreed. The agent only gave me twenty-five percent. I went off on her. I could not and did not think rationally. Here was someone trying to take yet another thing from me. There was no way she was going to take this from me without incident. Yet another door closed, and it was time to leave that office.

At what point do people take a look at you and see what you are going through? Where is the space for you to heal? You can't do it by yourself. People need people, but how does it come together? How can you find the right people to help you and the strength to let those people in? I didn't have the answers, but I knew one thing: my God would get me through this. I didn't know what my next step would be or what type of reputation I would have as I moved forward. It didn't matter. What mattered was surrounding myself with people who had compassion and respect for others. I wanted to coexist in an environment that promoted life and honesty with real people without cryptic agendas. During my stages of grief, I wasn't looking for people to feel sorry for me, only to understand that I had lost my child and it was going to take a lot of time, patience, and progress for me to even begin rebuilding my life.

I went back to the first real estate office to give it one more shot. By this point, Scotland had become a million-dollar agent. She took me back under her wing. It was slow, but we started to really bond and our friendship grew. She was a member of an organization called the St. Louis Chapter of The Drifters, Inc., whose focus was civic and community enrichment. I was impressed with how those ladies used their time and talents to make a difference in the lives of others. Their main focus was assisting high school students with college tuition. They held an annual scholarship fundraiser called the "Sweater Dance." I was still passionate about helping young people and the importance of a college education. I went to the organization's sweater dance and had a good time. They were such a strong, elegant, and giving group of ladies. The St. Louis Chapter of The Drifters, Inc. was the group to be a part of—a set of movers and shakers.

During this time, Whitney Houston's music had become an intricate part of my life. I had seen *The Bodyguard* with my ex-husband when it had been at the theatre. Still struggling with the death of my son, I had related to the movie in a different way than most, but I felt it deep within my heart. The lyrics to "I Will Always Love You" were words from the heart that could apply to many facets of life. It helped me realize that it was time for the girl in the mirror to move on from my marriage. I had some bitter pills to swallow and some I had to just spit out so I could find my way. Letting people go had become so second nature to me that I had the ability to accept the heartache at face value. My head and heart were programmed with the message that I had to wake up every day without my son, so I could walk away from anything or anybody. Hurting people hurt other people. It doesn't make a difference who they are, people will attempt to destroy lives and take away joy in many ways when they are hurting themselves. A time may come when you need to leave someone, but it doesn't mean that you didn't love them. The divorce was only one moment in time. The blessing is that God loves all his people, and he will always make it right for us. In a situation like divorce, we must forgive ourselves as well as others so we can move on to the next phase of our life.

Capture of Life

Time was moving along and things were going well for me and my grandson. He was almost 7 years old. Then it happened in 1998: two of my real estate closings fell through, and both the house and car payments were due. It was time for me to get a real job. How was that going to happen? I had been away from corporate America for so long. Every job opportunity was online, and I thought you had to know somebody to get a job. But I went old-school job hunting by pulling out the yellow page directory and searching for the telephone numbers of companies I wanted to work for such as AT&T Long Distance Company, Southwestern Bell Company (SBC), Union Electric, and Laclede Gas Company. I called each company to find out if they were hiring and what I needed to do. I later completed the applications and was given appointment times to be tested for the jobs. SBC and AT&T called me first, so I had to make a decision between the two. I took the job at AT&T's National Telemarketing Agency (NTA). Only my mother and sister knew that I had been offered a job with a start date. I called my brother Pookie Boy and asked him, "How would you like to work with your sister?" He said with his smart mouth, "I can work with anybody!" I went on to tell him that I got a job there. He said, "You have to past the test first." I told him, "I did," with a firm tone in my voice. Pookie

Boy responded, "You have to past the second test," as if I could not do that. I had become pissed at this point, so I raised my voice some and told him I had passed all the tests, already been interviewed, and would start on Monday! Then he was excited for his little sister.

Ultimately, God had placed me in this position as a way to rebuild myself. The most important person there was my brother, who had been employed with the company for a few years before I came on board. I had a nest egg put away to sustain me for some time, and I was still working as a realtor. Even though I was his little sister, Pookie Boy had always depended on me to rescue him out of situations, financial binds, and relationship troubles. Now I would depend on him to help me master this new job. Pookie Boy was aware that my vision was off and would be for the rest of my life. It always took a moment or two for my eyes to focus on something. The trainers thought I was a bit slow with computers, but I wasn't—I had been a main frame computer operator before the brain aneurysm. The glare of computer screens would hurt my eyes terribly, with or without glasses. My eyes had become sensitive to light, and movement of the residual blood would block my vision. I would have to wait a second for the blood to move out of my eyesight and my vision to stabilize before I could view what was in front of me. So I would sit with my brother before and after class so he could teach me how to navigate through the software applications. The six weeks of training had its ups and downs. There were times when I wasn't sure if I was going to make it. But, again, my most significant sanctuary was my brother, who would school me on what to do. He would come into the training room and drop off my lunch, so you know the other trainees along with the trainers took notice of the attention he provided me. A top performer at NTA, Pookie Boy was well respected by both his peers and management. Mayfair, one of the assistant trainers, took a liking to me. She told me that I was going to do well there. She complimented how I handled my customers on the phone and was impressed with my negotiation skills and professionalism. The NTA had a unique culture in and of itself; it truly looked for positive qualities and talents of its new hires so they could develop those skills from the beginning. "The Sky is the Limit" was one of the center's mottos.

There was a cultural organization at the NTA called the Black Alliance of Telecommunication Workers of America (Black Alliance, for short). The Black Alliance was a professional development organization that assisted with training and education to help you advance your career within AT&T Long Distance's NTA. Also, the public respected the organization for its civic and community involvement within the St. Louis Metropolitan area. The Black Alliance provided scholarships for high school students, workshops, and reading programs. The company also had tuition reimbursement after employees had been with the company for one year. This was the place to be if you wanted to elevate your career. I had always said, "If God ever blesses me with a job that provided tuition assistance, I would return to college and get my degree."

In mid-June 1998, I finally passed the final exam and phone test and was put on the floor to start taking calls. Mayfair, the training assistant, wanted me to join the Black Alliance and invited me to attend their black tie affair. However, it was on a Saturday I was scheduled to work from 2 to 10 in the evening. Since Mayfair had developed great relationships in the NTA, she was able to get someone to switch shifts with me so I could attend the affair. I completed my application and paid the fee to join, becoming an official member of the Black Alliance. This opened a window of opportunity for me that felt inconceivable at the time. Mayfair had a saying that would propel anyone to move forward; I knew it propelled me. She would say, "Handle your business" in a way that tickled me to death. Nonetheless, it was true; you needed to handle your business if you wanted to get anywhere in that company, meaning turning opportunities into sales and those sales into more sales. Although I dressed really nicely for the event, when I looked at the people around me, there was no connection between us other than we worked for the same company or we supported the same cause. This is when I saw that I had become stuck in time, in a period of life where I was unfulfilled. In that moment of time, I was able to see where I wanted to go, but I did not think I deserved to go there. Those people had their children. The event was a scholarship fundraiser, so everyone talked about their children's educational roadmaps and I could not. But God told me this is where I could make a difference in another young man's or woman's life so they could have a chance or second chance at life. He told me, "These children are a reflection of your son and what you wanted for him." This would become my way to give back and to learn how to live in the process.

We worked a lot of hours at the NTA because it was mandatory for us to put in a minimum of two hours of overtime every day. The money was good, and it forced me to talk to people. Through all the change and noise, I had still not been myself; I was still pretty withdrawn with no hopes of finding a happy-medium life without my son. In order to make my quota and keep the hardships of life at bay, I completely focused on my job. This by itself forced me to become one of their top performers like my brother Pookie Boy. I exceeded every last one of the metrics. I always had had a knack for quickly building relationships with people on or off the phone, which made my job somewhat easier for me. I did not talk on the side with other employees much, so this caused others to look at me as if I were standoffish, quiet, or withdrawn.

After I had been with the NTA for about one year, it became time for the Black Alliance Convention. We would be going to Baltimore, Maryland, and I had mixed emotions about the trip. But God did it again, placing a lady named Janice in my path in the company parking lot. She worked on the lower level of the building in the Easy Link department. After introducing ourselves, the conversation came up somehow about the convention, and she told me she was going to Baltimore as well. A God-filled woman, Janice was focused on raising her son and daughter. She had been divorced for some time but doing well. She was working on getting her bachelor's degree and told me about Lindenwood University and its accelerated degree program. We soon became friends and not just colleagues. Between her and Mayfair, my life could only improve from there. Again, this is how God will bless you with brand new friends that he wants in your circle. Since she was raising her son by herself, she would give me a lot of pointers on raising GDevonte Jr. and would counsel me in my low times. Janice was the influence I needed to get me to finish my degree. I enrolled in Lindenwood University, where the makeup of the accelerated program forced me into group settings; however, I still refused to talk about my personal life with others. The first essay I wrote was "Coping with the Loss of a Child," which my brother Sun June had advised me to write about. This was my real first step to healing.

Now I was ready to start going to events again—fundraisers, dances, award dinners, you name it. I was slowly getting my swagger back. My cousin June, who lived in Atlanta, was simply a jewel with a lot of patience. She took good care of me, instructing me on a lot of things that kept me out of a mental black hole. I did not own a pair of jeans when I started at the NTA; I just didn't wear jeans. However, I had to work a lot of weekends, so June went out and bought me jeans and blouses. For my first Drifters black tie event, she sent me a beautiful black sequined gown. An old schoolmate of mine, named Wanda, who was also a member of the Black Alliance, went with me to go shoe shopping for the event. I spent $260 on my shoes, which I still have to this day. It turned out to be a lovely night, although my date worked out well for that night only. I was still unsure of dating and how to date, but it was never an issue because my friend Scotland would find me an escort for our Drifters events. It was a challenge for me to enter life again, but somehow God made it possible, placing angels all around me to keep me from falling. My two "bestest" angels, as my son would say, were my mother and sister; they made sure I had all the love and emotional support I needed.

*****

I was doing pretty well and life was falling into place for me when my brother Snookie Boy passed away. This drove me nuts. How was I going to see my mother, knowing firsthand where her heart would be with the loss of her child? I questioned God again, wondering why I was put in this situation. I went over to my mother's house after Pookie Boy had called with the bad news. He had spent two weeks in Michigan with our older brother Sun June watching over him. Snookie Boy had been in a coma like my son had been. My mother had been too sick to travel, so Pookie Boy and Sun June had taken care of everything. Pookie Boy flew back to give my mother the news in person. He was at her house when I arrived. It was so damn hard to go through that door and be positive for my mother. I started to relive everything all over again. When our eyes connected, we saw into each other's hearts. I held my mother and let her cry. I flew back to Detroit with my brother for the funeral services. My sister stayed home to take care of our mother. It was heartbreaking trying to make decisions on who would stay and who would go to the funeral. My sister's heart was broken, but she always did what was best for our family without a second thought. Necie didn't get to say goodbye to Snookie Boy and neither did my little brother Ken or our mother. They did not get the closure one gets from attending a funeral.

There is always a pattern to life. Less than six months before Snookie Boy died, I had called him to tell him that he needed to get down here and spend time with our mother. I did not want what happened with him and Aunt Effie D to happen again with him and his mother. Snookie Boy had stayed with Aunt Effie D when my mother moved to St. Louis. She had felt he was too young for my mother to bring him with her to the big city. Aunt Effie D, our mother's great-aunt who had raised both her and Snookie Boy, had told him (before she went home to be with the Lord), "Snookie Boy, if you don't get down here to see me soon, the next time that you see me, you will be looking down over me in my casket." This is exactly what had happened. It had torn him apart like you wouldn't believe. Although it is always hard to see a man break down, it had been especially hard seeing my own brother fall apart. Snookie Boy had begun to drink a lot after returning from Vietnam. Then to make matters worse, he had been diagnosed with a disease associated with Agent Orange. I finally had been successful at convincing him to come down to see his mother. I even bought him a plane ticket to St. Louis. It had been the best week ever for our family. Snookie Boy had gotten a chance to spend time with his mother, his little sisters, and his brothers. He had cooked for his mother and cared for her that entire week. That week had felt like a lifetime to all of us, but what we hadn't known was that it would be the last time most of us would see him alive. Our mother would live less than nine months after Snookie Boy had died. It was too much for her heart. I know she grieved herself to death over her grandson Fatman and her son Snookie Boy. God pieces the blanket of life together as each of our parts are played out.

The quilt of my family's tree had started to unravel, the threads slowly coming loose. Sickness and death traveled like thieves in the night, as Aunt Effie D used to say. My mother's health had taken a turn for the worse. She had been diagnosed with chronic obstructive pulmonary disease (COPD) and emphysema and had been put on oxygen. She had to carry the oxygen tank everywhere she went. It had been unfortunate when my sister had gotten laid off work about six weeks before our mother's health really began to decline. But it turned into another blessing in disguise when she was able to be there to take care of our mother. Necie was always our family's angel of mercy. However, Necie had sustained serious injuries from her job, so caring for our mother became a real physical challenge for her. To help Necie and mom, I hired an aide to assist them for four hours each day. We all made sure our mother was well taken care of and gave my sister the assistance she needed to lighten her load. Necie was the main caregiver because the rest of us had to work to financially take care of both of their medical needs. We left no stone unturned when it came to the welfare of our sister and mother. GDevonte Jr. did his part too. At eight or nine years old, he could give his great-grandmother her medicine and change her oxygen tank better than we could. He loved her like no other.

Necie had to have surgery on her shoulder. GDevonte Jr. was out of school for the summer, so he stayed at my mother's house as he usually did while I went to the hospital to be with Necie. She had just come out of surgery and was headed to the recovery room when my cell phone rang. It was my grandson calmly explaining that my mother had fallen. He had called 911 and was waiting for the ambulance. I told him I was on my way. This was another surreal day.

A few months later, our mother's health took a turn for the worse. She had gotten to the point where she could barely breathe, even with the oxygen mask on. So my sister called an ambulance; they came and worked on her for a little while before taking her to the emergency room. The doctors put her on a ventilator and placed her in the intensive care unit. It was a long week as we watched her on that breathing machine. The doctors explained to us that she needed to be on the ventilator to slow the pace of her breathing and keep the fluid from building up around her heart. They said it would keep her in a relaxed state. Her children in St. Louis stayed by her side, praying together. By the end of the week, she was breathing on her own again and was taken to a regular room. We knew she was getting weaker, but we still had faith that she would be with us a little while longer.

As Mother's Day 2003 neared, my mother had lost quite a bit of weight and could hardly breathe. However, her mind was as sharp as ever. She had another attack where she could not catch her breath. My sister called an ambulance and then called me. I left work and made it to SLU before the ambulance did. They rushed my mother right into the emergency area and started working on her. We thought she was gone. She was in the hospital for Mother's Day. I got her the biggest basket full of assorted flowers and plants from Dierberg's, but it was too late to have them delivered to the hospital by Mother's Day. My mother and Aunt Effie D had always told us to give them flowers while they were alive so they could enjoy them. I was determined my mother would have her flowers on Mother's Day, so I had the store clerk help me put that big basket in my car. When I got to the hospital, I got a wheelchair to put the basket of flowers in. When I got up to my mother's room and she saw all the flowers, tears came to her eyes. She told my sister Necie to take her flowers home and make sure to water them every day. It was a bittersweet moment for us.

The doctors had told us they had done all they could do, and it was only a matter of time. My mother stayed on a breathing machine and was moved to an extended care facility. The doctors had given her only weeks to live. I was at work when something came over me. My stomach started to ball up in knots and I became ill. I explained to my boss that I had to take some time off to be with my mother. My mother had already told my sister, the doctor, and me that she did not want to go back on the ventilator, so we honored her wishes. But when I arrived at the facility, I heard my mother ask the doctor for some breath and not oxygen. My heart was broken in two because I knew only God could give her back her breath. He told me and my mother he was going to give her medication to make her comfortable. When he left, I explained to my mother that the doctors had told us she wouldn't be with us much longer and all they could do was make her restful.

My sister and my grandson came to the hospital the next morning. I left to go home and change. Necie and GDevonte Jr. fed my mother oatmeal for breakfast. By the time I made it back to the hospital, Pookie Boy and my cousin Connie were there. We began talking about old times. Then my stomach started to turn, and tears started to fall from my eyes. I walked over to my mother's bed and held her hand. Her eyes were closed. Necie told Pookie Boy, "Look at Debbie." They all got up and surrounded my mother's bed. My sister took her other hand, and I started to pray with all my being. By the time I was done praying, my mother had slipped away. She had taken her last breath and was gone. The doctor and the nurse came in. The doctor told us she had died, and another nurse came in to clean her up. Necie told them no, she would bathe her mother. My little sister bathed our mother, combed her hair, and put lotion all over her body. Necie stayed in the room with my mother for a while. I finally told my little sister it was time to go. We had done everything we could for our mother, and we had to let her go. I called my pastor and the funeral home. We waited until they got there. My pastor prayed for our mother before the people from the funeral home took her body.

We sent my mother off in style. She was buried in a navy blue dress I had bought her a few years before her death. Her casket was pink, with a spread of pink and white carnations covering it. She had on a heart-shaped corsage with red roses from GDevonte Jr. My sister and I wore navy blue dresses and pink corsages. Our brothers and my grandson wore blue suits, white shirts, and pink neckties. My mother looked more beautiful than ever before. My oldest brother Sun June said, "She had such a radiant smile on her face as if she were happy to see whoever had come to get her."

*****

With only a few weeks left in the semester for my classes, I had an essay due. The instructor knew my mother had passed away, but he had the nerve to tell me I could not miss class. Although I could come in and leave after turning in my final essay, I didn't even know how I was going to finish this doggone paper. My good friend Janice stepped right in to coach me through. Calling me on the phone that night, she threatened me in more ways than one, telling me I was *going* to finish writing that essay. Janice stayed on the phone with me while I typed and cried. Eventually, I got it done and turned in the essay, passing the class. I only had two quarters left to go before I would have my bachelor's degree. My grandson would see his grandmother walk across the stage, earning both a bachelor's degree and, later, a master's degree. I wanted to be an example of every good thing possible for him. I wanted to be his inspiration to succeed in life.

So Amazing

Soon another life-changing surprise occurred in March 2005 when the NTA laid off everyone, giving us a two-month notice. You know God will continue to make up for lost time in many ways, but you will have to work your butt off to earn his blessings. GDevonte Jr.'s mother decided he should come live with her. My grandson had been with me since the death of his father. That was the only life my grandson knew. My intention was to stand in the gap for my son and by all means necessary take care of his son. I was a constant help for her and would intervene when necessary. I spent quality time with him on my days off and made sure that he had all he needed and then some. My heart went out to his mother because I could see that she had not dealt with Fatman's death. I took her to the cemetery once to show her that he was gone and that she needed to move on with her life. There was nothing I wouldn't do for her because she was my grandson's mother, and if it took every breath I had, I would keep that door open for my son's sake regardless of the situation.

It was a long haul, and GDevonte Jr. experienced great pains and hurt going back and forth between my house and his mother's house. I had gotten hired at another communications company right before the end of the two-month period. Then the lady from human resources called me to say they had rescinded the offer but would contact me as soon as possible. Thank God I had some money saved, and I thanked him for his mercy. I could not for the life of me understand how they could send me a job offer in writing and then call me to take it back, but that's corporate America for you.

I waited two weeks, during which time I had to take immediate custody of my grandson. We spent a lot of time on our knees praying, asking God to give us strength and to open doors. Then I received a call back from the same company letting me know I had the job, but it turned out to be one of the most stressful jobs I had ever endured. A different culture existed there, but only on one floor of the building. It seemed as if I were working in a dark cloud. When you stepped from the 8th floor to another floor, it seemed as if you had entered another dimension; the employees were happy and loved their job. A lot of the employees in my department were not happy. I felt lost in this unfamiliar environment. I had one goal, and that was to raise my grandson. I had to make sure GDevonte Jr. could get to and from school on time and make all his doctor appointments. Since I worked full time, my sister stepped in to help me when I was unable to take off work.

Throughout these transitions, I was active in church and loved going to worship service and Bible class. I continued to be surrounded by guardian angels. I had my big brother Pookie Boy to protect me, my little brother Ken to make sure I was straight financially and emotionally, and my baby sister, who would listen, pray, and be there every time I called. I had a circle of friends who supported me: my prayer partner Priscilla "PJ" Demps, who taught me prayer will go through walls; Louise T. Wilkerson, who provided precious life lessons to my grandson; Cheryl Darough, who gave me motivational tapes to keep me going while I worked out on my treadmill and who made me a customized calendar with all of my family's birthdays and special days to keep me focused; Pastor Douglas M. Parham and his wife, Sister Agnes Parham, who came to the house to pray with us; and friends like Lynn Williams, who would be there for me without me needing to ask and would do anything to help. There was none other than the Reverend Dr. James E. Lacy and Sister Doris M. Lacy who taught me, "I Have a Faith That Can Conquer Anything." It was a long five years for me and GDevonte Jr. My cousin Connie would pray with me and sometimes just plain go off on me to get me through the rough times. Then there was the Quiet Storm, my friend Lashonda Wright. She had been on my team when we had worked at the NTA. Our friendship continued long after we had lost our jobs. She would listen to me cry as I wrestled with the struggles of raising my grandson. Last but not least, I cherished the friendship, sisterhood, and life experiences shared before, during, and after my tenure as a member of the St. Louis Chapter of The Drifters, Inc. All these relationships helped mend my heart.

Soon God brought me to a place of peace during my grandson's senior year. He went to his homecoming dance, a layer of guilt dropped off; he had his senior pictures taken, another layer of guilt dropped off. Looking for his tux for the prom, joy burst within my heart.

After I paid his senior dues, waves of gladness circled through my head. When he walked across the stage, shaking the principal's hand to receive his diploma at Midtown Technical County High School, oh my God, the fruits of the spirit surrounded me and a peace came over me that I had never felt before. God had afforded me the opportunity to fill in for my son, and I could let him rest now. The long road was now counted as all joy. I could not change my son's death, but I could make that difference with my grandson. The true essence of giving back means to give of yourself for the greater good of others. Standing in place for my son meant I had made many sacrifices for my grandson's well-being. We had made it. To that end, when my grandson walked across the stage and received his diploma, I knew my son and my mother were smiling down on us saying, "Job well done."

However, thoughts and feelings of hurt and missing my baby came to the surface; I was unable to hold them back. Feelings are always there, but they hold a special place within your heart, soul, and mind. You learn ways to control the temperature of the agonizing pain until you arrive at a quiet place to let them flow again. The feelings must flow or the sense of loss will consume you to the point that you have no ability to respond to anyone. It is easy to fall into a cloud of depression knowing your child won't return home in this lifetime. Now, as my grandson reached the milestone of graduation, I was unable to hold back the tears for my son; I did not even care who saw me crying.

My grandson had told me one day when he was sixteen that he had been placed in a position where it seemed there was no way out. Although the pain and hurt were so deep, he could not allow anyone to see him cry, so he cried within. This had to have been one of the most painful times in his life. Whenever I reflect on what my grandson had told me and in the way his heart had been pierced, I recall those moments when I have cried motionlessly on the inside, with invisible tears rolling down the innermost part of my heart. This had been when he discovered, "But God"—that only God has the ability to step in. God then replaced the pain with peace and washed away his tears. This is something that I will always believe: you can't take a child that is accustomed to sleeping in a bed and teach him how to sleep on the ground, but you can take a child that has learned to sleep on the ground and teach him how to sleep in a bed. We set standards for our children, always reminding them of the different worlds people live in within our world and teaching them to always be cognitive of who they are and where they came from.

I had an assignment to write a poem for my Humanities cluster in undergraduate school, and I called it "Crystal Clear." This poem came together for me because I needed to know God loved me, and I had to accept and love who I had become as well as find a shelf within me to lay my pain upon.

Crystal Clear

The sun shining through the trees
I am free
The bluest sky
I am free
The crumbling sound of leaves beneath by feet
I am free
I can see the stars and the moon
I am free
A release of past tolds
and embrace of new learns
I am free
This love is for me
It is crystal clear
Yes, I am free

Miss Me Now

Seasons fall in the order of spring, summer, fall, and winter ... yet it can snow in the spring, temperatures drop in the summer, and temperatures can rise during the fall and winter. Fall and spring have a lot in common. During the fall, the leaves change into magnificent colors then fall from the trees, only to become dry and crunchy under our feet as we walk over them. Spring brings us beautiful flowers that last a while, only to fade away with the next season. The same happens with our lives: events come out of a season. Beneath all the beauty lies the hurt, controversy, denial, and questions as to why all over again. Yes, it gets better in time, yet you perpetually relive the season, that moment of time, as if it were today. The thought continues, *do I deserve to be happy?* The birthdays and holidays are for family and children; where do I fit into the framework of this life? Remembering my son's death brews sorrow that lies in the innermost part of my heart and soul. I lost my son, which, again, is not supposed to be the natural order of life.

Now as destiny has filled the details of this season of my life, I have learned how to articulate and express the life and death of my child to others. These are stepping stones in my life and moments that will never be replaced. By God's grace, I turned grief into power and moved forward with my life as I searched the mystery of how my son knew death was upon him. Right after he had died, my sister had found a poem that my son had written about his life. He summed up his life in this poem as well as how all of us would be affected by his death:

To my Boys on the set

How many day did we walk the set, how many nights did we just sit to see days & nights past? And how many things we did th were not right?

And how many days and nights we heard our mothers pray and cry? And how many years has it been that I have been walking this set of life?

What did I gain in this walk of life - a son that I will never know or watch him grow, a girl that I have left with a heavy load.

How many loved ones have I left behind that will only see me in their minds.

Why couldn't I just take time just to listen to that old gal of mine wh she told me about this Man she kn that walked the set, but with different rules? A set that gives life and not death, gives hope and not hate, a set that gives joy and peace at no price, the set that gives eternal life.

Turn

Now that I walk this set that I chose alone hoping that my homies will see the light, and take time to sit and listen, so they won't have to walk this road alone.

Love,

Gary (Fatmo

Our children can see things we cannot because they are still our arrows in life. On the night of Whitney Houston's death, God spoke to me and revealed to me why he had taken my son. It hurt so badly when I saw the news flash on CNN, "Whitney has died." No more than fifteen minutes earlier, my friend Gil and I had had a conversation about how hard it is for people to stop using drugs, and we had talked about Whitney.

My grandson, who was away at college, called and said, "Grandma Debbie, Whitney just died." This was the second semester of his freshman year. Amazing, as young as he was, he knew how much I loved her and had an understanding of what her music meant to me. My sister still talks about how my grandson had placed himself right in front of my mother's television set with his yellow sleeper on listening to "I Will Always Love You" as he swayed from side to side in this deep trance; only an angel's voice could do that to a child. Every time he would hear Whitney's voice, he would run through the house to get to that TV so he could see and hear her sing. Her music had a profound impact on my grandson as a small child, and her music, especially this song, had become a spiritual connection between me and my grandson later in life. One Christmas he bought me her *Waiting to Exhale* CD and the movie. Even then, God had a plan for her and a hand on my grandson.

After I was done speaking with my grandson, I called Gil back to tell him about the death of Whitney, and I was crying. I had prayed for a long time, hoping she would recover from her addiction and that God would heal her broken heart. My friend said to me, "I don't understand why people go to drugs and not God." I told him what I felt about Whitney's situation as well as others. I believe with all my heart that Whitney, like my son Fatman, did lean toward God, but their journey had to be traveled, and in the process, they did not know how to turn it over to God. You must have the will to live, and when the will to live is gone, this is when God calls them back home.

As she reached out to God, Whitney Houston recorded a song, "I Look to You," and my son, Fatman, wrote the poem, "To My Boys on the Set." These are true testaments that they were saved and did not lose their salvation.

Let God and Live Life

The true elegance of life is God's unchanging hand. He will never put on us more than we can bear. God will place people in your life to help you turn the pages. He has kept me humbled, and my life's blessings are right in my face today. As life takes its course, there are mothers like myself, my mother, and from all walks of life who have traveled the road of coping with the loss of a child. It is a lifelong journey, but through God's daily grace and mercy, love of family, support of friends, and our children as our guardian angels, we can embrace those memories of them and keep them close in our hearts to receive the joy that only the Holy Spirit can give us. We can cope, and we can live life again.

My son lit up my life, and my grandson GDevonte restored my faith, brought me new hope, and gave me a reason to continue to fight the good fight and live. Now the birth of my great grandson, Romeo, has created a new light in my life.

"I am with you always, even to the end of the age" (Matthew 28:20 NKJV).

Conversations Along the Way

My grandson was coming home for the weekend, so I picked him up along with a couple of his college friends. This weekend was special for us. He was coming home to celebrate his twentieth birthday, and we were both excited. He was even more thrilled because the St. Louis Cardinals were in the last game of the World Series that day. Imagine, he was in absolute awe, them making history on his 20th birthday!

During the conversation about baseball, one of his friends told us he loved basketball, but, unfortunately, he said he didn't play it anymore. He told us how when his dad had come home from prison, he had bought him new tennis shoes and they went straight to the basketball court. Then he said, "My old man died, and I have not played basketball again." I paused for a moment before speaking because I didn't know if he was aware that my grandson had lost his father. Another repercussion of dealing with the loss of a child is the unseen domino effect. I was in the car with two young men, hearts beating loudly, both quietly mourning the loss of their dads. How do they cope with it? I wondered if he had ever told his mother or if she had ever acknowledged that he had not played basketball since the death of his father. Did he ever tell his mother or anyone else, and if he had, did he receive an encouraging response? I believe he felt safe in talking to me because he did know my grandson had lost his dad too. In the end, I said to him, "Your father desired for you to play basketball; it was a father-and-son bond between the both of you. This would enable you to have the peace and joy your father aspired for you to have."

This is where you want to be the piece of fabric that helps mend a broken heart, and you pray for the proper words to say so another person can heal and find a place of harmony within. He did not say anything, but I do believe it gave him something positive to think about, and hopefully, he will play basketball again because it would aid him in putting back together the pieces of his life.

*****

One day, one of my coworkers had on a pair of FILA tennis shoes. When I saw them, I went into a trance, staring at those shoes. It had come to me that my son had worn those shoes back in the eighties and early nineties along with his Guess tennis shoes. It was like the past had made its way to the present. I looked at him and told him the story of my son and those tennis shoes. In speaking to him, you would have thought that it had happened just yesterday. I went on to tell him about the outfit I had bought him for his last birthday: a short-sleeve polo shirt, a pair of Guess khaki shorts, and a pair of Guess tennis shoes. The R&B group Boys to Men, who were in the same age group as my son, had worn similar outfits back in those days. It came to my mind how handsome he was and how bright he was. For a split second, I smiled; it felt like he was right there with me. Only soon the smile would be erased by reality.

*****

Around 5 in the evening June 28, 2013, another one of my coworkers, Cocoa, told me she needed to talk to me about something. She said, "Ms. Debra, I did not mean any harm last week when you asked me why was I so quiet. Did you hear about the four shootings in Bellefontaine last week on the news?" I told her I had not. She went on to explain that it was her cousin Tony who had been killed. She told me Tony and another guy had been shooting from under a car while getting shot at, and he would have lived, but his girlfriend got shot twice, and he came out from under the car to save her, and that's when he got shot. She continued that while she was at the wake the previous night, she had thought about me. Cocoa said her cousin was only twenty years old, but what got to her the most at the funeral was when this little boy ran past her, his mother calling out his name. She had looked and asked, "Who is he?" One of her relatives told her he was cousin Tony's two-year-old son. As Cocoa relayed the story, tears came to her eyes and I became teary-eyed as well. I thought to myself, "Another child without a father, another mother without a son, another broken branch of life in a family tree." She went on to tell me her deceased cousin's mother had asked Tony's girlfriend if she could take her grandson home with her. Then the girlfriend had said she had to leave; she could not take it anymore.

After telling me her story, Cocoa asked me, "What are they going to do?" When she looked at me, I saw the hurt and fear of uncertainty. I also sensed she wanted something from me, not just for her, but for her cousin's mother. Answers, answers, and more answers. This is what we all want. *Why, why my child, why me, what did I do, what did they do, and most importantly, how am I going to go on without them? What is going to happen to their children? How will I tell them as to what happened to their mother, father, sister, or brother? When will be the right time, and how much of it will I tell them?* Only God knows, but he will prepare a time. It may not be a good time, and it may be in a no-choice situation, but it will be in his time.

I wrote my memoir to bring about an openness to everyone who will meet an unforeseen event in their lifetime. Some may only have one challenge to overcome, while others may experience multiple encounters to be overthrown. In having been a teenage mother, my desire is to help other teens as well as young adults be mindful that sex does not validate who you are as a person and you do have other options.

Grandma Debbie is a living atlas for grandmothers who have or will have to intercede as caretakers for their grandchildren. Know that you can be the exclusive difference-maker in the lives of your grandchildren, and as grandparents, we are the village of wisdom, love, and understanding.

The essence of Grandma Debbie's life lessons is like a bridge over troubled waters to aide in the journey of healing, to get past the heartache, anger, pain, grief, and loneliness that embodies the emotional experience of losing a child. Through the tailwind of faith in God, forgiving yourself and others, rebuilding your family, and reaching deep within yourself, you can extend love to others. There is no exercise better for the heart than reaching out and lifting someone up. This can only be accomplished by working in alignment with God and family.

"Great things start happening,

Good things start getting smooth."

By Gary Romeo Cannamore III,
my 6-year-old great grandson

"An Art of Love" by Fatman

Photos

Critical Moments in My Life

Necie, me, and Ken the day of Daddy's funeral, 1969

My freshman year at Beaumont High, 1970

A moment in time, 1977

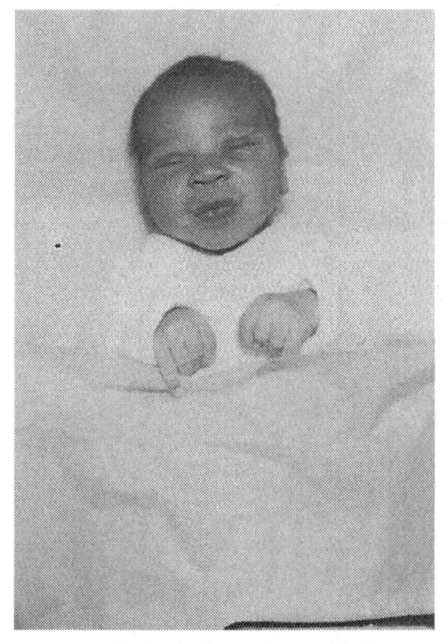

My baby's first day of life

The last picture taken of me before I suffered the aneurysm, 1986

Fatman's Life with Family and Love

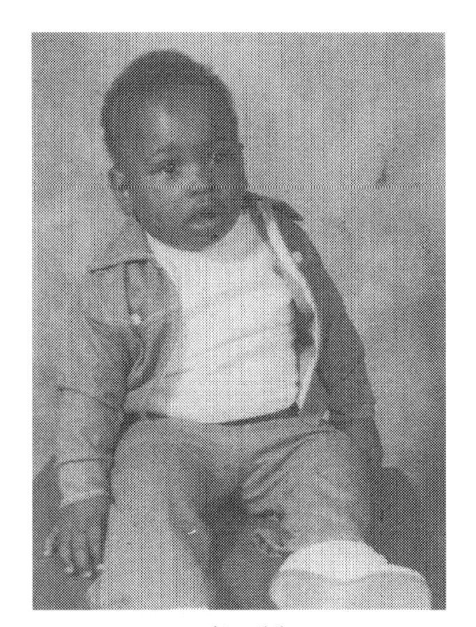

6 months old, 1973

3rd Christmas, 1976

Fatman and his uncle Ken sitting on my first car, a 1973 Mustang

4th birthday, party in the backyard

Mother and son, ages 20 and 5

Necie and her precious Fatman, 1977

Easter, 1979

Fatman and his first lady,
Grandmother Mutt, 1980

Me and my sister Necie, 1981

School Days

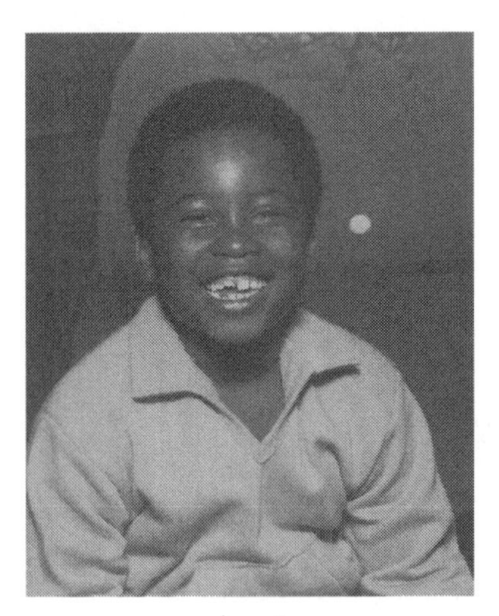

Age 5

Age 7

Age 9

Personality

Age 16

Prom night

Passing the Torch to the Next Generation

Mother and son, 1987

Fatman and his son

Celebrating Education

Rejoicing after earning my bachelor's degree, 2004

Receiving a master of business administration (MBA), 2006

Acknowledgments

To my parents, Laura Mae (Mutt) and Oscar, for giving me a name to be proud of, to live up to, and for instilling values of life and family in me at an early age.

To my Heavenly Father, who has and always will be the rock of my foundation.

To the pillars of my life, my one and only sister, Denise, and my brothers Oscar Jr., Clemmie, Rommie, and Kenneth, for loving me no matter what, when, where, or how. I cannot thank you enough for your support.

To Garey L. Watkins, M.D., without whom I would have never come this far in my recovery. You've made all my accomplishments possible.

To all of my past and present friends and the strangers (angels) who have positively influenced me during this journey of my life.

To my husband Gelhaar, for the love and support he gives me to continue my journey.

A special acknowledgment to my son, Fatman, the breath of my life; my grandson Gary, the tower of my life; and my great grandson Romeo, the wishing well of my life.

About the Author

Debra Cannamore Lee, a native of St. Louis, is an active member of the community, having been involved with Mathews-Dickey Boys' and Girls' Club, the Campus YMCA at Washington University, and the St. Louis Chapter of Drifters, Inc. She's currently a supervisor of clinical support at a major health care company. She enjoys writing, speaking, dancing, traveling, and spending quality time with family and friends. A daughter, sister, mother, grandmother, great-grandmother, and wife, Debra passionately lives life to the fullest. *Grandma Debbie* is her first book.

To learn more, visit Debra at www.grandmadebbie.com.